HAMMOND PUBLIC LIBRARY
W9-BMO-935

Keep Those
Volunteers
Around

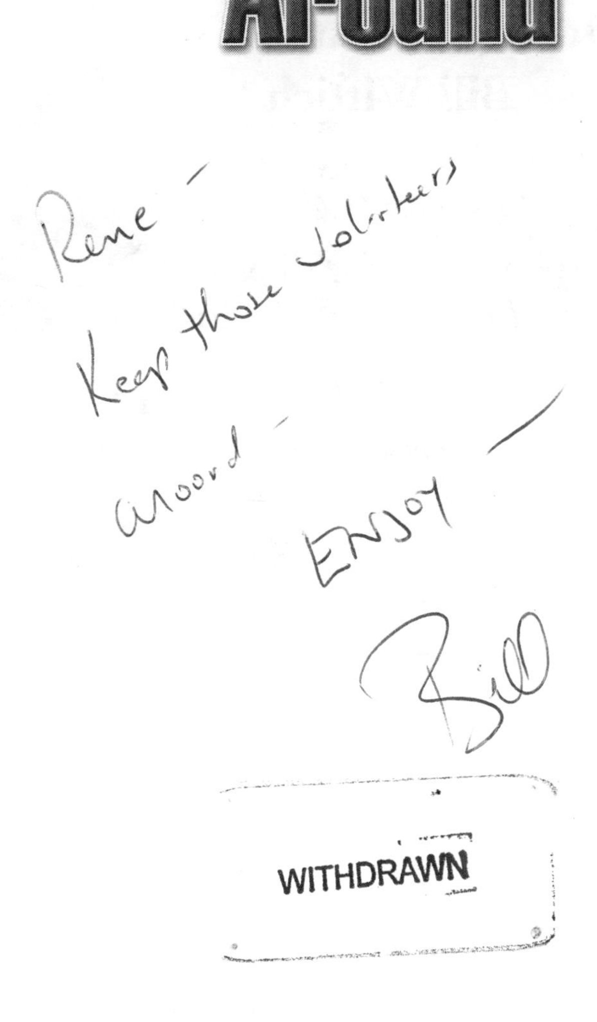
Rene -
Keep those Volunteers
around -
ENJOY
Bill
WITHDRAWN

Other Publications By
Bill Wittich

The Care & Feeding of Volunteers

10 Keys for Unlocking the Secrets to Excellent Volunteer Programs

Model Volunteer Handbook

A Collection of Volunteer Forms

A Dozen Easy Tips to
Excite, Inspire, & Retain
Your Most Valuable Asset...
VOLUNTEERS

Dr. Bill Wittich

Knowledge Transfer Publishing

Manufactured in the United States of America

Library of Congress Catalog Card Number: 2001118628

ISBN: 1-928794-11-4

Cover design: Ad Graphics, Inc.

Editor: Andrea Pitcock

Knowledge Transfer Publishing
3932 Cielo Place
Fullerton, CA 92835
Tel: 714.525.5469
Fax: 714.525.9352
Knowtrans@aol.com
www.volunteerpro.com

To our two daughters,
Andrea and Tami,
who have always given us
their support and love.

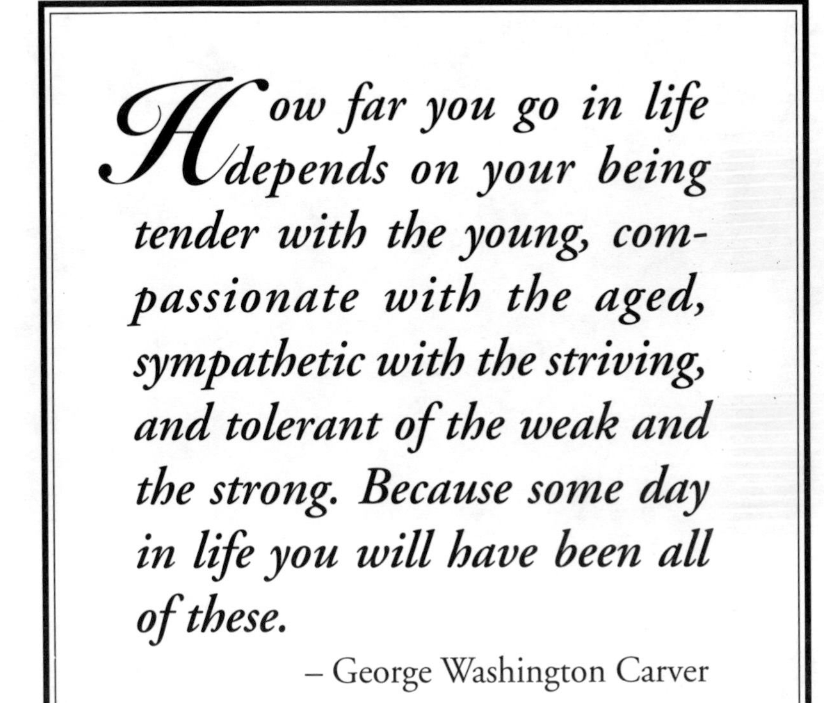

How far you go in life depends on your being tender with the young, compassionate with the aged, sympathetic with the striving, and tolerant of the weak and the strong. Because some day in life you will have been all of these.

– George Washington Carver

Contents

A man can succeed at almost anything for which he has unlimited enthusiasm.

– Charles Schwab

INTRODUCTION

As a volunteer coordinator, I think I spent most of my time going down to the local shopping mall to put up beautiful posters, then running down to the city hall and placing my brochures on the front counter. I then had volunteers sitting at the shopping mall meeting and greeting the people walking by and asking them to volunteer. I would talk to all the local service clubs, the Rotary, Jaycees, Lions and in fact I spent many lunch times giving pro bono presentations as a recruiting tool. I went to all the junior and senior women's clubs finding volunteers. All of this worked very well. We had a steady stream of new volunteers coming in the front door of our office. But we also had a steady stream of volunteers going out the back door. We had a problem keeping those new volunteers. It seemed as if most of the new volunteers got really excited about volunteering and then in two months, that excitement began wearing off and out the door they went. I had a major retention problem. Let me tell you a story that I think will make a point about retention.

My wife Ann and I love to eat. Recently we have learned to eat healthy, but early on we were fast food junkies like most of the world. We had a local pizza place, a nice one with red and white tablecloths, low lighting and friendly wait people. We went there every Friday night to order our pizza, salads, and a bottle of red wine. Without fail, if it was Friday night, we were at our favorite table in the corner. The owner of the restaurant was a gentleman who we also saw there but never had the opportunity to meet. He was kind of loud and was certainly a Pittsburgh Steelers fan. We could hear his conversations about his team. This particular Friday night we ordered our standard fare and when it arrived it was awful. The pizza was simply overcooked and looked like a small tire sitting on the plate. We called our server back to the table and suggested that they try it again. The owner overheard us suggest that they try the pizza again and he came right over to our table. In his very loud tone of voice that we heard before, he proceeded to tell us directly that he would not charge us for the pizza, but that we should not return to his restaurant. We were shocked and, as you can imagine, we did not return there again. But I bet that if we did sneak into that restaurant and listen to the owner, he would be talking about how tough it is to continually find new customers! He failed to understand that it is easier to keep those good customers that you have instead of always looking for new customers. In many ways, that is exactly how I acted as a volunteer coordinator. I was always looking for new volunteers, but I didn't take the time to work at retaining the ones I already had in my organization. This book will give you a dozen quick techniques for doing just that, keeping the good volunteers that you already have on the volunteer roster.

The techniques this book will discuss will involve everyday common sense, the kind that everyone has but seldom uses in the workplace. These techniques are the nuggets that will make people feel appreciated, will motivate them to continue volunteering. This book will explore those reasons why people volunteered in the first place. It will look at various forms of communication and listening skills and a multitude of recognition suggestions. Robert Wendover, in his little book *2 Minute Motivation,* says it best when he states, "no person excels in relationships without the help and support of others."[1] This book, therefore, is mostly about those relationships that you build with your volunteers. Relationships start with getting to know the volunteers intimately and understanding what makes them tick as a volunteer. What do they like to do for their assignment and what types of rewards might spur them on to success? This book is based on the simple premise that volunteers will stay in organizations where they are given support, shown appropriate recognition, and managed well. The culture of organizations using volunteer help will vary widely, from places that consider volunteers to be full staff members to those that literally ignore the volunteer efforts. This unique culture must fit the volunteers in order for them to stay long term. We will discuss this culture and the techniques in this book will help you match your particular organizational culture to the volunteers.

The steps we will be discussing will involve taking ownership of keeping your volunteers and realizing that keeping those good people around is your first step to success. Your focus needs to be having the commitment to finding out what is making them start thinking about leaving in the first place. It's talking to your volunteers, asking them on a daily basis about their assignments, how they are feeling about their volunteering. It's continuing to show them that you care about them, that you value the work they are doing. It's using common sense in placing the right people into the right jobs. It's realizing that everyone has skills and talents but not everyone "fits" into every work environment. Finding this "right fit" between the organization and the volunteer is critical to the volunteer's success, and therefore their retention.

Retaining volunteers is becoming a major concern. But it does match what is happening in the paid workplace today. Managers are pointing out that the average workplace loses half its employees every four years. In fact, more than half of all employees think of quitting within a year, and even in the world of professional human resources the common thought is one of replacement rather than retention. The best people managers realize that it is the people who keep us in business. We are in the service business, serving those various clients that we have, the parents in a school, the children that the volunteers work with, the patients in the hospital, and the citizens who live in your city. It is key to realize that people stay longer at places that care for them, take the time to get to know them and recognize their efforts.

We need to understand, as we begin to talk about retaining volunteers, that zero turnovers are impossible to achieve.

Volunteers will leave for a variety of reasons. Many of them good reasons that are out of your control. Their spouse gets a job offer in another city and they move. They decide to return to full-time work and cannot find the time to volunteer. They retire from their jobs and start traveling. They return to the university to start a new life direction. There is nothing you can do about these situations. In fact, some turnover is healthy for the organization. New volunteers will bring fresh ideas and approaches to your place.

Even if some turnover is unavoidable, and that it's even healthy to have some turnover, it's really critical to get a fix on exactly what is going on inside your organization. Just how many volunteers leave each year? Is that number about average with other volunteer organizations? Is it about average for the paid workplace? What are the key reasons why people leave their volunteering? We will examine all of these thoughts in this book.

But even after we look at the reasons and accept them as things to work on, it is really the volunteer manager who keeps people or loses them. I always think of my mother-in-law, Cecelia. She worked all her life as a dedicated nurse and loved every day of it. When she retired and moved back home to Atlanta she started volunteering at a local hospital. She looked forward to this new opportunity but almost from the start she found conflicts between the volunteers and the volunteer manager. Even this wonderful woman, strong and willing to help, found herself leaving the hospital because this manager was simply not a people person. The manager simply did not know how to care for the volunteers.

We have thousands of dedicated hard-working volunteer managers in the workplace. But even these wonderful caring people sometimes lack the tools and training in people management. The new volunteer manager may never have had a day's training in these concepts. So often people are asked to take over the manager's position as an extra assignment. They are simply given one more briefcase to carry home at night. A case of more work for no more pay. All of us need training in the concepts of coaching, motivating, facilitating, and cheerleading volunteers. In my seminars, I always tell my attendees that they need to learn to wear a variety of new caps in order to be successful. They need the caps of cheerleader, coach, and motivator. This book will give you these new caps to wear and help you find the strategies to keep your volunteers around.

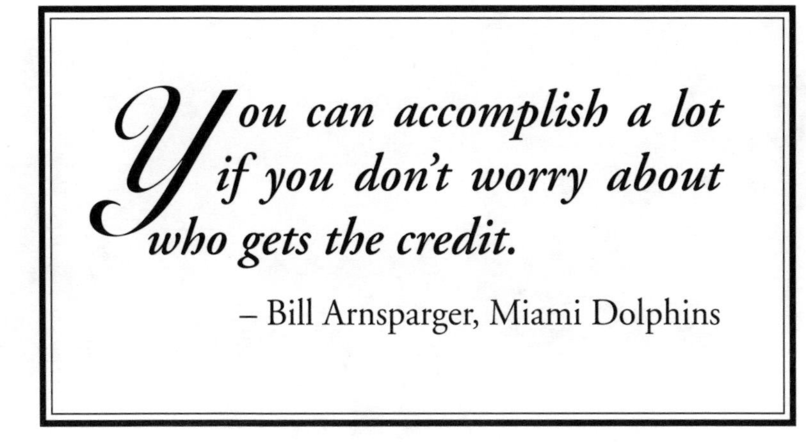

You can accomplish a lot if you don't worry about who gets the credit.

– Bill Arnsparger, Miami Dolphins

Chapter One

Connect with Your Volunteers

Life is what's happening while
we're busy making other plans.
– John Lennon

Everyone wants to connect with somebody. Volunteers, just like paid employees, desire a feeling of belonging to the culture of the organization. It is the volunteer coordinator's job to insure that this connection occurs. But, how do you encourage this connection between volunteers? Sometimes it requires you to just pause for a moment and walk around your volunteer place. As managers we get caught up in the hectic atmosphere of budgets, client problems, and tasks that scream for attention. We need to step back and catch our breath, and savor the moment. Richard Carlson, in his classic best seller, *Don't Sweat The Small Stuff,* calls it "learning to live in the present moment." He says, "This quality of being in the moment has far more to do with what's going on in your mind than on what's going on in the office."[2] The key is to be with the volunteer when you are with the volunteer. Nothing disturbs people more than the person talking to them who is not really there. We have all talked to people at a party who are much more interested in the new arrivals or where the boss is than talking to you. As Carlson says, "It's the small things," and this is one of them that really breaks the connection.

Jim Harris, in a book titled *The Employee Connection* gives us a couple of hints about connecting with our people, both staff and volunteers. He suggests that we challenge ourselves to connect in the moment with a different person every day. He also suggests that we open a conversation with a simple statement of how you feel at that moment.[3] You might say that you feel excited or tense about something. Offer one or two reasons why, and then ask if they feel the same. You are encouraging them to be bold enough to share in the moment. By putting yourself out there first and sharing your feelings, it usually helps to open up the other person's feelings. Sometimes it pays to lead with a personal weakness; because I am only 5'6", I will sometimes tease about the fact that I can't seem to reach the top shelf where the supplies are kept. This self-deprecating humor will help to break the ice and start conversation flowing.

All of us have a need to feel important at times, or at least to think that what we are doing has importance. How do we help to give this feeling to our volunteers? Maybe we could start conversations with more "you" than "I." It is a natural tendency to talk about what we are up to in our lives and to not spend much time asking about their lives. When we are asked for our opinion, it gives a feeling that the other person cares about our thoughts. Alice Potter in her book, *Putting the Positive Thinker to Work,* says it well, "…if you give others what they want, they will give you what you want."[4] What you are looking for in your conversation with the volunteer is simply a chance to get to know your volunteers better. Sometimes this can be achieved by trying to see things from other people's view. I know that this requires asking questions, and then listening to their answers. This has been difficult for me, as I always seem to want to get right back into the conversation with my opinion. Henry Ford, always a wise man, may have said it best when he stated, "If there is any one secret to success, it lies in the ability to get the other person's point of view and see things from his angle as well as from your own." It has been difficult for me to avoid interrupting the person that I am having a conversation with. It seems that they are taking so long to conclude their thoughts and I could help by just breaking in now! All of us resent the person who doesn't really listen and we really get upset by the person who doesn't let us finish. Richard Carlson says, "I also realized how destructive this habit was, not only to the respect and love I received from others but also for the tremendous amount of energy it takes to try to be in two heads at once!"

All people like to be asked for their opinions. Don Blohowiak in a neat little book, *Think Like Einstein, Create Like Da Vinci, and Invent Like Edison*, gives us a critical thought about being an effective boss. He says, "You need not be a power station of new ideas, just a lightning rod for them."[5] The value-adding manager knows that everyone is capable of suggesting better ideas. Usually just asking volunteers for their thoughts about a problem is, in itself, both a compliment and a morale builder. Besides, it will probably truly give us another view of the problem facing us. One idea that I like to use is an informal meeting with new volunteers, after about three weeks, where I ask them for their observations about the organization and particularly the volunteer program. It is always amazing to me the new insights that I gather from these "new kids" about how we might improve the flow and culture of the organization.

Tom Peters has the right idea when he suggests that the best management tool might be to learn to manage by wandering around. He refers to it as Managing By Wandering Around (MBWA).[6] Give up memos and e-mails and go out and interact with your people. It's much faster and much more effective. You also have a chance to see how things are really working at your place. You might want to ask their opinions during those wandering visits as well. Maybe the question, "What would happen if we approached it this way?" will start meaningful conversation. Questions simulate thinking. Questions that are open-ended, and not simple yes or no questions, will allow for a more stimulating conversation. Martin Sandler and Deborah Hudson in their book, *Beyond The Bottom Line*, talk about Martha Baker from the San Diego Zoo. At the zoo, managers learned on the run. They rarely had a chance to sit down, because as soon as someone inquired about a project, somebody would get up and say, "Let's go check it out." Along their way they greeted every employee they met. The zoo managers were constantly aware of the visitors around them, asking them what their experiences were.[7] This wandering around is a strong form of management and one that the employees are bound to notice. These managers could receive their information from memos, but how much more effective if they see the results themselves. The simple advice for volunteer managers is to get out of their office and roam around.

Never tell people how to do things. Tell them what to do and they will surprise you with their ingenuity.

– George S. Patton

Chapter Two

Give Fast Feedback

You get the best out of others when you give the best of yourself.

– Harvey Firestone

One of the strongest frustrations that I have experienced from volunteers is when I fail to tell a volunteer how to improve their performance. Too many managers are literally fearful of attempting to improve the performance of a volunteer. It's as if their volunteer will break down in tears at the suggestion that they are not doing the job perfectly. The truth is that all volunteers want to do the best job for the place where they volunteer. But all of us need feedback from our boss in order to continually improve our performance. This feedback can come in many ways, in coaching, in performance reviews, and over a friendly cup of coffee. I remember a boss that I had who conducted performance appraisals of employees as if they were little children going to face the strong father image. Everyone hated these sessions, including, I am quite sure, the boss delivering them. They were conducted in an environment of fear, and the employee expected punishment and demotion as a result of the evaluation session. Too many bosses are forced to conduct evaluations without any training in how to conduct performance reviews.

I do not use any of those words, performance reviews, performance appraisals, or evaluations. I call this process feedback. Feedback should be a two-way street, as you discuss the volunteer's performance, they should give you feedback about how well they feel the organization is treating them. I always conduct this feedback session in an informal setting, usually over a cup of coffee in the lounge or on the front steps. It is a learning experience for both the volunteer and the manager. It should be positive in nature and, in fact, you should start the session with positive comments about the volunteer's performance. Everyone does things well and does a few things not well. We can all improve and we are always continually learning. Push the learning part in your feedback session.

Feedback should be done both formally and informally. The formal session happens once a year. It should be discussed at the new volunteer orientation and during training. It should not come as a shock to the volunteer a year down the road that you are going to evaluate performance. The process and sequence of feedback should be outlined in a training session and the forms to be used should be given out and discussed. Informal feedback occurs as you walk around your facility and observe the volunteers working. The simple stopping by their workstation and placing your hand on their shoulder and saying "good job" is part of this process. I love the feedback process because it gives me one more opportunity to say "thank you" to my hard working volunteers. The leader must continually give informal feedback on-the-run, quick evaluations of work in progress. Don't wait until the work is completed to become critical or praising. How many times have you worked on a project and received no feedback on the quality of your work? No comments on how well you did or how you could have improved it? No positive pats-on-the-back to spur your motivation along? Some volunteer coordinators paint clear pictures of what they expect but fail to measure the volunteer's performance against those standards. Check how you feel when you slave over a project and receive no feedback at all. It takes away all the good feelings of accomplishment and motivation. This situation causes the volunteer to lose respect for the coordinator and to lose interest in the task at hand.

The informal feedback starts with the first day that the volunteer is on the job. It starts as you coach the volunteer by suggesting an alternate way of doing their job, or when you watch them lose it and ask them to join you for coffee and give them a pep talk. It continues as you observe them, or even hear positive comments about them from a client, and you make a few notes for their file. I like to carry a small post-it pad with me on my daily rounds, and I leave positive short notes on their desk or workspace to compliment them on something I saw or heard. Copies of these thoughts go into their files that I will review before I prepare for their formal feedback session. I call these personal notes my "love notes" since they usually reflect my personal thoughts about their positive performance.

The formal feedback sessions are held annually, since I believe that the life of a volunteer is literally about one year. Every year your volunteers reach a point where they will make a decision about their future. After a year of volunteering, they will consider whether they have met their goals completely. All volunteers come to you with goals that they would like to accomplish. When they have been performing their tasks for that year, they will feel good about the work they have accomplished. As they work on the same task for a year, boredom might set in, and a job change might be healthy. One of our jobs in conducting feedback is to ask if this volunteer is ready to move on to another assignment within the agency. You do not want what happens too often in the workplace, workers are trained and perform well but do the exact same thing for years and reach a point of boredom. Change may be scary but it may be the best thing for some of us. If the volunteer says that they are ready to try something new, suggest changes to their agency assignment. One of the keys to retaining volunteers is insuring that they remain interested in their assignments. But remember that many volunteers will want to stay at the same task for years, and for many volunteers, it's working with the same people that they love. If that's the case, just let them sign on for another tour of duty.

The second possibility is that the volunteer needs a change of volunteer place, that they may be ready to volunteer somewhere else. I had a situation recently where my volunteer and I were sitting down for feedback and I asked him the question as to whether he had someplace other than ours where he needed to be volunteering. His eyes filled with tears and I was shocked. I had asked a question that must have hit a hot spot. He said that his son was now in Pop Warner football and he was committed to coaching for them every afternoon. He also said it was bothering him because he didn't know how to tell me that he had to leave my place. He said he loved his volunteering with us but that his son was simply more important to him right now. He asked, "How did you know that I was ready to leave?" It was an easy question. His performance had already gone down hill as his enthusiasm had begun to shift to his upcoming coaching volunteer work. There is nothing worse than a volunteer who has quit already in their mind but has not yet left the agency. Their heart is no longer in their volunteering, but they don't know how to tell you that they have something else they need to work on.

The third possibility is to offer the volunteer a promotion. Offering the volunteer a more meaningful work assignment might mean being in charge of the black-tie dinner committee or taking on the leadership of your meals-on-wheels team. This used to worry me. I was offering more work to a volunteer who was already performing very well. Wouldn't this burn out this volunteer? Is it right to push an excellent volunteer to take on additional responsibilities? The answer is yes, in many cases. If you tell the volunteer exactly why you are offering this new, more leadership-oriented assignment to them, it will be flattering. Say it like this, "Mary, I would like to ask you to consider taking on the volunteer director of the hospital gift shop for the next year because you are so organized, you get along with everyone and you are so positive." When she hears your request, followed by your honest appraisal of her abilities, she will feel good about being asked. Then she will give you an honest decision as to whether this new opportunity is something that she feels she would want to consider. You must be aware that she may be in love with working in the gift shop but has no desire to be the boss. She may only have enough time to work one shift a week, not the multiple shifts required of the manager. She may be a perfect salesperson, but not a person who wants to attend other meetings and organize schedules.

James Belasco, in his book *Teaching the Elephant to Dance* says, "If you don't measure it, people will know you're not serious about delivering it."[8] This really means that you don't hold an annual review of the volunteers performance and put it aside for another year. It means you pay attention to performance on a daily basis and give coaching or praise continually. If you think of a basketball coach, you realize that they really only do two things in their jobs. They praise and work to improve performance, that's it. In fact, the coach gets paid for the performance of his or her players. If his or her players do not win, the coach will be looking for a new coaching position. Can you imagine a coach holding a review of the player's performance at the end of the season rather than all season long? That is exactly what some volunteer managers do; they do annual reviews of each volunteer rather than conducting on-going feedback sessions. Blanchard, in the classic book, *The One-Minute Manager*, calls this the 'leave alone-zap' style of management. He says, "This is what we often do with new, inexperienced people. We welcome them aboard, take them around to meet everybody, and then we leave them alone.[9] Not only do we not catch them doing anything approximately right, but periodically we zap them just to keep them moving."

Some managers do not even conduct annual reviews; they ignore the whole process of performance review. Most research of employee performance problems illustrates that the cause is either poor or no feedback from managers. Feedback is mostly coaching, watching volunteers perform and giving supportive feedback aimed at improving the performance. If feedback is poorly given, or not given at all, the result is a volunteer who continues to perform poorly. Many times the volunteer manager is afraid to give feedback because they feel it will hurt the feelings of the volunteer, or they are afraid to confront the volunteer with negative comments. A few managers will tell you they have no time to conduct feedback sessions, or that they themselves have never been trained in how to conduct feedback sessions. If the manager has never been coached himself or herself, they have no role model for outstanding coaching.

Most outstanding athletic coaches learn real fast that yelling, screaming, berating the player does nothing to improve their performance. For too many volunteers, the only feedback they really get is criticism. But criticism is ineffective at coaching them to peak performance, and it can lead volunteers to hide mistakes and avoid contact with their managers. Rick Pitino, in his book, *Lead To Succeed*, says, "Your underlying message—one that must be constantly reinforced—is that you care about the people you are leading. You value them. You care about them as individuals. You care about their work environment. You care about their success."[10] Pitino suggests that using praise, encouragement, and recognition, which includes some form of personal touch, is important. All coaching requires rewarding people, making them feel important. Sometimes the best form of coaching is letting your volunteers know the unseen results of his or her efforts. If you hear positive comments from someone, let the volunteer hear them from you. Spread the good thoughts!

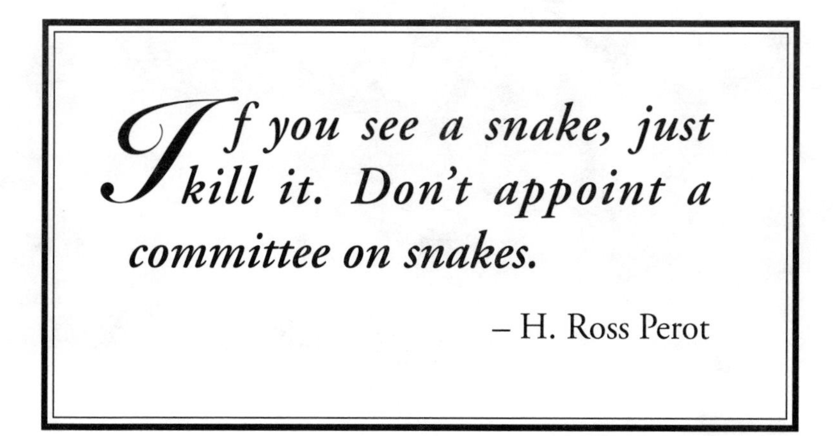

If you see a snake, just kill it. Don't appoint a committee on snakes.

– H. Ross Perot

Chapter Three

The leader finds the dream and then the people.
The people find the leader and then the dream.

– John Maxwell

Somehow people think of volunteers as people who care but really can't get the job done. The whole concept that we hear so often that they are "only volunteers" says it all. Even volunteers have been heard saying that they are only volunteers, therefore don't expect too much of them. Or the attitude that the volunteer is not getting paid, so don't expect a professional attitude or performance. This is absolutely silly. Look at college sports players. They don't get paid, but they will play their hearts out on the football field or basketball court. Why doesn't the college player say, "Well I am just a college player, don't expect too much from me until I get a big salary in the pros"? You and I know that this attitude would never get them to the professional ranks. Also, the fans don't pay high dollars for college stadium fifty-yard seats and then say, "Don't expect too much because they are only beginners." So why do we allow this minimal expectation from our volunteers? It's our job to raise the bar and begin to expect excellence, to commit to excellence.

Lou Holtz in his book, *Winning Every Day*, gives it to us directly when he says, "Leaders must challenge and inspire. I know that many people today believe that demanding excellence is politically incorrect. We are supposed to accept whatever an individual gives us as the natural expression of his ability and not pressure him or her by asking for anything more. Nonsense."[11] Our job as volunteer coordinators is just like the college coach, that is, to find and develop the best volunteers we can. Our job is to encourage our players and help them reach their goals. Every volunteer arrives at your front door fired up to perform a job that will make a difference. They have a burning desire to create change for people. Read the mission statement for your agency. Isn't that what it says it will accomplish? And those volunteers come in to do these tasks that will make that difference. So what happens? Many times it is the lack of leadership on the part of the manager and their staff that deflates that excitement. Holtz uses the example of General Patton who, when quizzed about the ability of his army to finish one battle, march one hundred miles and then fight another encounter in less than forty-eight hours, said, "That's what we're in business for." Every leader must think that way.

These high standards start with us. We must know and understand what we are there to do. We have a job to perform that makes a difference in people's lives. We use volunteer staff to accomplish this task. We could not get it done without them; none of us have enough paid staff to accomplish our goals. Our volunteers must be continually motivated to continue their daily chase toward getting the work done. That's when we must put on our coach's cap and start to work. The volunteer manager must have the traits of leadership and be the kind of person that people want to follow. I have seen many definitions that try to explain the difference between management and leadership, but the best, I think, comes from Warren Bennis. Warren is a professor in the Leadership Institute at USC. He says that "managers do things right, but leaders do the right things." When you work with volunteers, doing the right things is critical. This involves selecting the right people, continually motivating them, and assigning them to the right tasks.

Volunteers want a leader who they can trust. A leader who quite literally "walks their talk." A leader cannot be a person who says one thing but does another. Volunteers look up to their volunteer leader; they expect to see commitment and honesty in them. A leader that talks about putting the client first, but fails to do so, is far more likely to be judged harshly by their volunteers and clients alike. People expect the leader to be committed to the mission of the organization and to the volunteer program. Sometimes it seems that the volunteer manager has too much on their plate or may not really understand why someone volunteers. In fact they had never volunteered themselves. This is a recipe for disaster. People do not follow uncommitted leaders. Commitment inspires and draws people to you. They will follow you if they believe that you believe in the cause.

John Maxwell, in his classic text on leadership, *The 21 Irrefutable Laws of Leadership*, talks about the law of buy-in. Maxwell says, "People don't at first follow worthy causes. They follow worthy leaders who promote worthwhile causes. People buy into the leader first, and then the leader's vision."[12] Think about your own past experiences in business or in a nonprofit. Didn't the person that you respected as a leader become the person who influenced you to become even more involved than you ever thought you would? Maxwell says it so well when he states, "People want to go along with people they get along with." As a leader though, it is not enough that you have this vision and a good cause, you must become a better leader. This is a never-ending task. Studying leadership means watching fellow leaders in action, it means reading books about and by leaders, it means attending seminars and viewing videos. Leadership is a skill that can both be learned and then continually refined. It is the key skill of the volunteer manager, oops, sorry, of the volunteer leader.

Champions aren't made in gyms. Champions are made from something they have inside of them—a desire, a dream, a vision. They have to have lasting stamina, they have to be a little faster, they have to have skill and the will. But the will must be stronger than the skill.

– Muhammad Ali

Chapter Four

Empower Your Volunteers

If you want a successful business, your people must feel that you are working for them—not that they are working for you.

– Sam Walton

Ever have a boss who used the "D" word? You know the word, it's delegate. It didn't take us long to understand what delegate meant. You were given a job that you knew the boss didn't want to do. Delegation never did really work and it certainly did not motivate, since you were usually doing the other person's work for them. The technique that does motivate is empowerment, and it's very different from delegation. Empowerment is sharing the responsibility and authority necessary to get the job done. This concept derives itself from outstanding customer service places such as the department store Nordstrom. The process involves giving the front-line worker the decision-making ability and responsibility to satisfy the customer. Betsy Sanders, in her book *Fabled Service*, says that, "The key to providing fabled service is to get decision making done as close to the customer as possible."[13] We have all attempted to return an item to a retail store only to have to talk with the sales clerk, then the department manager, then to another person, each of which would pass the buck to the next person. It's been said that the more people you have to talk to in order to handle a transaction, the less likely you are to ever be satisfied. Therefore, empowerment means that you have to trust your clients to the front-line people, volunteers, and you have to equip these people to do the job.

At Nordstrom, the employee handbook says it all:

WELCOME TO NORDSTROM

We're glad to have you with
our company.

Our number one goal is to provide
outstanding customer service.

Set both your personal and
professional goals high.

Nordstrom Rules:
Rule #1: **Use your good judgment in all situations.**

There will be no additional rules.
Please feel free to ask your department manager, store manager, or division manager any questions at any time.

Their single rule, to use your good judgment in all situations, is the key to empowerment at Nordstrom. It says that we trust the employee to make decisions that benefit everyone involved. As Sanders says, "There is an 'absolutely no-problem attitude' on the part of Nordstrom salespeople; they take the challenge of sending the customer away delighted, very seriously." Empowerment has to start by selecting the best people for the job and then training them properly. I refer to this technique as the two T's of empowerment. The first T is training. You must train your volunteers to do things your way, that is, the way the agency does it. The second T is to trust these volunteers to get the job done in their own way. Once someone has been properly trained to perform a task, you can trust him or her to make slight alterations to the timing or procedure. But if they were never shown how to perform they are truly "a loose cannon." They will try and may, or may not, accomplish the task in a satisfactory manner. Empowering your volunteers really means filling them with power. They can then use this personal power to be their best, to try their hardest to accomplish their tasks. From the Nordstrom annual report comes this statement on service;

If service at your company is to be legendary,
it must be everybody's business.

There are two job descriptions: Those who take care of customers and those who take care of caretakers.

Your expectations of the people who serve the customer: Good judgment, positive attitude, passion for the customer, desire to be part of a winning team, willingness to give their all.

Your people's expectation of you: All of the above, plus meaningful work, respect, the opportunity to share the big picture, a clear set of standards, ongoing training, appreciation and recognition, responsibility for decisions, freedom, and support to be their best.

Think about these two sets of expectations. First the expectation of the volunteer. You expect good judgment from your volunteer. You work during the selection process to pick volunteers with a positive attitude. You develop, during your training, the passion for the people your agency serves. You coach continually to instill a strong feeling of team and partnering. And you know that these volunteers exhibit a willingness to give their all.

What about the volunteer's expectations of you? You give all volunteers meaningful work to perform. You share all information about their tasks and give them a big picture view of the agency. You have developed an on-going training program. Recognition in a spur-of-the-moment way shows your volunteers that you appreciate their efforts. And you continue to give the volunteers responsibility as the tool that allows empowerment to flow within your organization.

Robert Spector, in his recent book, *Lessons from the Nordstrom Way*, captured the essence of this empowerment when he said,

"The fact is: You empower people by giving up the power yourself." Nordstrom gives the people on the sales floor the freedom to make decisions, and management backs them on those decisions. Spector relates the use of this principle in the non-profit work at an organization titled Feed the Children. Feed the Children "wants to push the decision-making responsibility and authority down to the lowest level possible." Spector quotes Feed the Children's vice president Paul Bigham as saying, "It's a cliché, but we never lose sight of the fact that it is essential to what we do. Our charge to the people who work for Feed the Children is this: 'you can do anything you want as long as you stay within certain parameters. Don't go out of those parameters. Inside those parameters, I don't want to hear from you. If you don't feel comfortable in making the call, go up-line and let someone else make the call.'" [14]

This statement really speaks to trusting the people you hire as volunteers and giving them the freedom to make decisions on the spot. It teaches the volunteers that empowerment comes with accountability. We must also understand that the risk in empowering volunteers means that mistakes will be made and our approach must be to accept errors and learn from them. As you move the responsibility for some of the day-to-day decision making down to your front line workers you are accepting that your role as manager will change. Are you willing to trust your volunteers to make good decisions? Did you spend the right amount of time selecting the right people? Are you conducting adequate training? These questions must be answered in the affirmative in order for empowerment to work. Do you believe that responsibility and control belongs at the top of your organization? If that is your fundamental belief, then just say no to empowerment. Don't create an illusion of team and partnership that ultimately you will not fulfill.

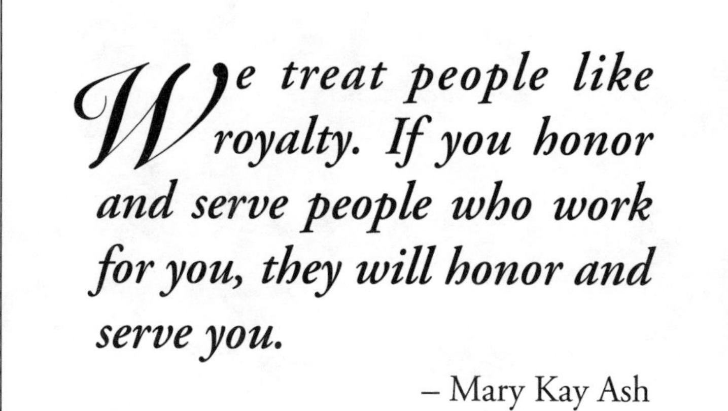

We treat people like royalty. If you honor and serve people who work for you, they will honor and serve you.

– Mary Kay Ash

Chapter Five

Hire the Best

You're only as good as the people you hire.
– Ray Kroc

The single most important thing we do is to select the best people for the job. Picking the best volunteers and placing them in the best assignments that match their skills and interests is the answer to success. Everything is secondary to picking the right people. There is always an assumption that the manager can take anyone and with a little coaching, turn him or her into a winner and the team goes home with the trophy. Isn't that what happens to the Little League team down the street? All the local kids apply for the team, some who can play ball and some who can't. Then the coach, who is told by the parents to play all the kids, is expected to turn out a winning team. We know this is fantasy, and it is fantasy to assume that just any volunteer could run the gift shop or deliver meals for your meals-on-wheels program. This is the equivalent of warm body recruiting, where you simply have a volunteer walk in the door and the next day they are working. We know that a team in professional sports is only as good as its players. This is just as true in volunteer management. David Thielen, in his book, *The 12 Simple Secrets of Microsoft Management* says, "It's irrelevant what you think the quality of your employees is. What matters is what the level of quality truly is."[15]

This is not to say that the quality of staff is all that counts. Bad managers can still create problems. Bureaucratic procedures can mess up the flow of work and even cause volunteers to leave your agency. Our point here is to come up with a procedure for conducting good interviews. The process at Microsoft is worth considering. They have the employees in the group hiring for a position, interview the candidate. If we follow this model we would allow the volunteers in a group to interview candidates. For example, in a meals on wheels unit, the current volunteer drivers would interview all new candidates for driver and help make a decision about which people to hire. The manager would then conduct a separate interview and using the volunteers' comments and their own reactions to the candidate would hire the new volunteer drivers. You will find that the current drivers are more concerned about the quality of the new volunteer than management is and, with a little training, can do a better job of making that determination because they are closest to the job. As an aside, it also builds the self-esteem of the current crew because you respect them enough to help you make a critical hiring decision. Thielen says it best. "Hiring the right person is the most critical decision a manager makes." No matter how desperate you are to fill a position, no matter what the consequences, do not compromise. Spend the time necessary to make the right selection. The quality of your staff determines if you can succeed. It's that simple.

Hiring volunteers is a two-step process. First is the need to check their backgrounds, to help eliminate the risk involved with having volunteers in your workplace. Second is the need to insure that the person selected has the skills and interest required in the position. The first step requires that you, the manager, check this background yourself and, upon your approval of this person from a risk management standpoint, you involve other staff in the interview process. During the interview process, try to spend as much time as possible with each potential volunteer. Skills are relatively easy to develop, and knowledge is easy to acquire. But more difficult is changing someone's attitudes. So, go for people with positive attitudes, personalities that are bright, and people who can relate to you and your colleagues. Experience counts, but, first and foremost, is the desire to succeed.

Zig Ziglar, best selling author of *Over The Top*, says that it's your attitude, not your aptitude, that will determine your altitude.[16] This attitude means that you are willing to see the good in things, to see an opportunity when an obstacle faces you, to treat others the way you want to be treated, to encourage others when they need support, to have something nice to say, and to be willing to maintain your attitude every day. Tom Peters says it so well in his book,

Reinventing Work: The Professional Service Firm, "Everyone says, 'People are our most important asset.' In a professional service firm... PEOPLE ARE OUR O-N-L-Y ASSET."[17] If you are serious about finding volunteers who will serve your clients, you start with people who are willing and able to make it happen. Hiring well means being highly selective. One critical skill is the volunteer's people skills. Chip Bell and Ron Zemke, in a light hearted but hard common sense book, *Managing Knock Your Socks Off Service,* talk about staff being good at handling their own emotions, calm under fire, and not susceptible to "catching the stress virus from upset customers."[18] Our volunteers are truly front-line workers, in a customer service sense, and they do interact with your customers.

These customers are the citizens relating to neighborhood watch volunteers, the patients and family in a hospital setting and the students in a school classroom. What do people whom your volunteer serves really want? Jeffrey Gitomer in his book, *Customer Satisfaction is Worthless,* says they want "communication, attitude, reliability, and empathy."[19] Gitomer gives these examples of these four key traits of the person who serves customers:

Communication – "Let me know what I need to know when I need to know it."

Attitude – "Happy, eager, willing...prepared to meet my needs."

Reliability – "Consistent...be there when I need you."

Empathy – "Understand me and my needs. Give me your commitment."

Martin Sandler and Deborah Hudson in their book, *Beyond The Bottom Line*, give an example of nonprofit customer service at the Children's Museum of Indianapolis. "...kids are the customers, the museum's reason for being; and kids make up the core of the volunteer staff." One volunteer stated that, "The training I received taught me more than how to guide people through the museum, it taught me how to deal with people's concerns, how to explain things clearly and, best of all, how to help make the museum a better place for kids my age."

Hiring volunteers is easy, anyone can do it, but hiring the right volunteers is another matter altogether. Your place is very different from the nonprofit down the street. Some volunteers that would thrive in your place might not last a day next door. Some volunteers thrive on pressure, others want a quiet place. One volunteer likes it fast, another slow. Some volunteers love children, others adults. One person is a people person, another is very task-oriented. Your job is to locate the right volunteer for your particular environment and culture. Avoid the first warm body through the door method of recruiting. If you can't get the right person, don't take anybody. Selecting the wrong volunteer will make your life, and work, harder and more frustrating. Spend the time to interview the prospective volunteer and then let your staff help you make the final decision.

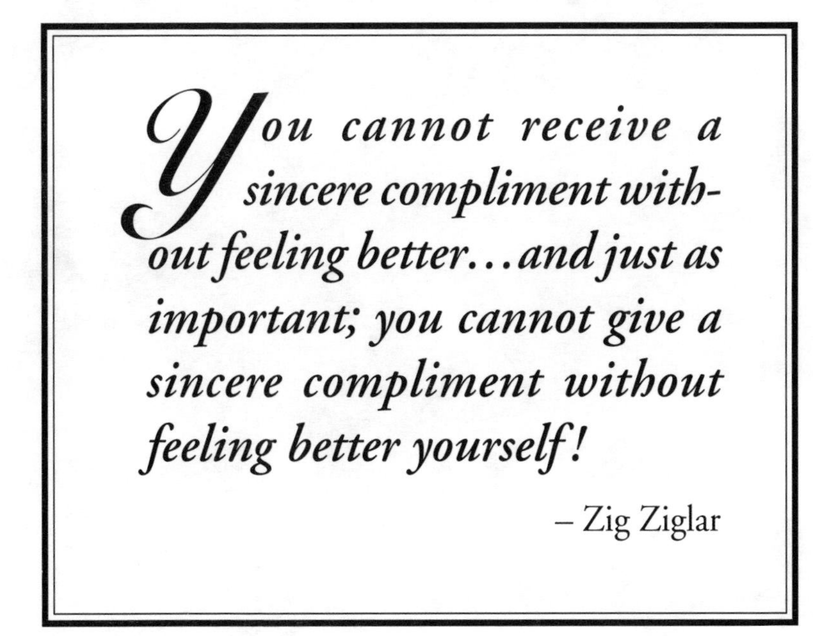

You cannot receive a sincere compliment without feeling better...and just as important; you cannot give a sincere compliment without feeling better yourself!

– Zig Ziglar

Chapter Six

Simple observation suggests that most of us are trinket freaks—if they represent a genuine thanks for a genuine assist.

– Tom Peters

You can call it recognition, rewards, praise, whatever, it all works. People love to have someone recognize the fact that they are appreciated for having done a good job. There are as many ways to recognize volunteers as there are volunteers. What works to make one volunteer feel good does not work on the next volunteer. There is no such thing as too much praise, as long as it is sincere and delivered in the right way. The driving rule is to simply use common sense in conducting recognition. Do not ever embarrass a volunteer through recognizing them. Do not recognize someone who has done nothing to deserve it.

Ken Blanchard says it best in his classic text, *The One Minute Manager,* where he tells us to catch the person doing something nice and praise them for it. I call this recognition that is done on the spot, "Spur of the Moment Recognition." You should not wait to praise someone until you have a collection of things to say thank you for, just follow the Nike lead. Just Do It, the Nike theme, is how we should conduct recognition. Whenever you observe or hear about something the volunteer has done, go over to them and make a big deal about it. One of the keys to good recognition is to recognize volunteers often and when the spirit moves you. In other words, if you see a volunteer being particularly friendly to a guest, tell the volunteer how it makes you feel and how that act of theirs will make a difference around there. This spur of the moment form of continual reinforcing recognition will set awareness in your place that people do care about the small things.

Also reward volunteers for specific things that they do. You should reward for performance and excellence. When you give recognition, you are setting a pattern that the volunteer will repeat in the future. Like children who are praised for a good deed, all of us tend to repeat actions that brought us positive attention. You should give attention to those acts that are positive and when you praise the person for it, mention the act as part of the praise. Being specific and mentioning the task that you are praising lets them know exactly what behavior deserves the recognition. Don't ever become a "throw-away thank-you person." That's the person who runs around saying thank you with no apparent reason to say it. My wife and I volunteered at a place in Los Angeles where we would show up on Saturday mornings and help. Whenever we arrived, the volunteer coordinator would run right over and give us a handshake and say thank you, thank you. This was repeated every time a volunteer arrived and became slightly humorous to the volunteers. At one point we were enjoying a cup of coffee in the break room when one volunteer could not hold it back. He said, "THAT WOMAN, has no idea what we do, in fact she doesn't even know our names." She was a throwaway thank you person. She felt that thanking people was a good idea and she did it every time a volunteer showed up for duty. My advice, be sure that when you thank a volunteer it is for some specific thing that they did that is big enough to deserve the attention.

Thank yous should be done in a variety of ways, in written form, on the phone, in person. It really does not matter, and they all work. There are informal and formal times and ways to reward volunteers. The informal ways and times are those spur of the moment times when you simply observe someone or hear about something someone did that was positive and uplifting. Formal recognitions include the annual awards luncheon and the recognition meeting where the fund-raising awards are presented. Many of us were trained that recognition should be in the form of a handwritten card and mailed in a white linen envelope with a first class stamp on it. Don't get me wrong, that is fine, but there are hundreds of recognition opportunities everyday that don't require that formality. I observed one of those moments recently when, after having lunch with a volunteer director and driving back to her agency parking lot, she observed a volunteer's car. She had talked at lunch about this volunteer and had mentioned how effective the presentation he had made to the city council had been, and how it will help the program in the future. Upon seeing the volunteer's car, the director got out of her car and reached into her purse and took out one of her business cards. She wrote a short note on the blank side of the card. It said, "Thank you, Joe, for a wonderful and highly effective presentation last night. It will make a difference in the city council attitude concerning our organization. You made a difference, thank you." That was so effective because it followed our rules for recognition, it was very specific by mentioning exactly what the volunteer had done that deserved praise, and it was done spur of the moment. If she had waited until the end of the year banquet, it would have lost its impact. I know that that little business card note which she had put on his windshield, under the wiper blade, will go home with him and be shared with his family.

Recognition can be done privately or publicly. Some volunteers get very embarrassed being praised in front of others and, for them, a private praising with something that acknowledges their good deeds, that they can take home or place in their office, is helpful. They will still enjoy sharing these notes or awards with their families. I remember one volunteer, a lady named Mildred. She was the classic people-person, loved to be around people. She had a group of friends that she always wanted to volunteer with on the same shift. She was the ringmaster, the real leader of the band. When recognition time came, it was obvious to me that she deserved special recognition for her hours of tireless work. But I knew that bringing her up on stage at the annual banquet would not be a good idea. True affiliators do not like to take the center stage because they feel their friends deserve the glory as much as they do. I could not ask all of her friends to receive equal awards or it would equalize the recognition, and Mildred was truly the responsible one. So I took our monthly newsletter for that month and devoted the entire front page to her story. I even included a few photographs of her at work. As I expected, when the issue hit the streets, she was upset! But the reality of the situation, according to her older son, was that she was very excited by the article, since it mentioned her friends, and even showed them in the pictures. Mildred ended up asking for six extra copies of the newsletter to send to family members. It had worked, but at the time it felt risky. The real danger, though, is to continue to ignore these hard working volunteers just because they act like recognition would be embarrassing. But for most volunteers it would be less effective to praise them in private. It is the public arena that brings those feelings out. It also lets all the volunteers see that you do recognize outstanding performance and that you are willing to stop for a moment and praise that performance.

Remember, you only thank someone when they have done something deserving of praise. You do not thank a volunteer for coming to work, or for sitting there all day. You thank them for that particularly difficult call that they just had on the domestic violence hot line. You thank the volunteer for taking the extra effort with that child who had a really tough time with the other kids, and they talked the child out of tears. But, you must be wandering around your place to be able to catch these things. You should also be willing to praise those actions that are brought to your attention by another staff member or volunteer. Sometimes just stopping a volunteer in the hall and saying, "Andrea, you always are in such a positive mood. Just today I heard that you showed Judy how to understand that File Maker Pro computer program. I know it was driving her crazy and you simply made her day more fun by being so positive. Thanks for that." It's the little thoughts expressed out loud that make it work. What you as the manager think, does not help to praise the volunteer. You must make them aware of your positive feelings toward their act. And if you follow up with a written note, it's even more effective.

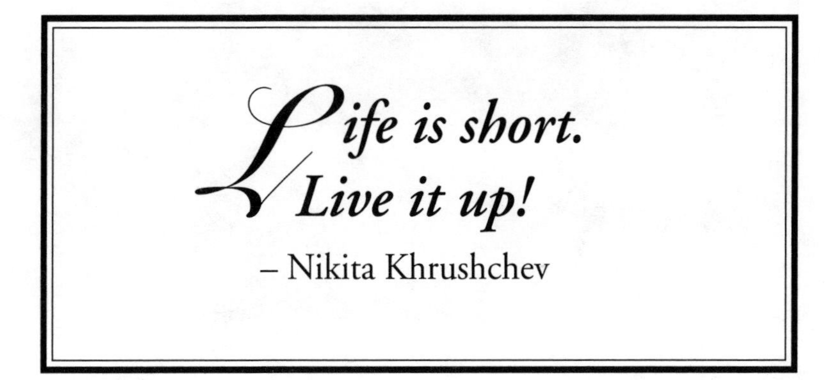
Life is short.
Live it up!
– Nikita Khrushchev

Chapter Seven

Humor is a spontaneous, wonderful bit of an outburst that just comes. It's unbridled, it's unplanned, and it's full of surprises.

– Erma Bombeck

Research shows that people who have fun at work are more enthusiastic workers. Enthusiasm leads to increased productivity, a positive attitude about their jobs and higher odds that they will stay at the place. In other words, a fun environment will lead to increased retention of volunteers. A serious, even boring workplace is what too many volunteers have experienced at those places where they earn their living. Most workplaces are serious and dull. Too many bosses think fun equals unproductive time, but research is showing us the opposite. Those dull places lead to people searching for places that know how to lighten up.

Just remember that what is fun to one person is not fun to another. You will find that some volunteers would feel very uncomfortable in a fun environment, while others would literally come alive. This speaks to the culture of the organization. That's why we conduct interviews and walk-a-rounds with new volunteers, to see if their personality fits the organization. We cannot be all things to all people. If we have a light, fun, relaxed atmosphere, some will think we are not business enough, while others will eat it up. Don't worry about this; just create an atmosphere that fits most volunteers. And don't assume anything. Try it out. You will be shocked at how seniors will enjoy the fun setting even more than those twenty types that started the fun flowing. Fun can involve painting and designing the room as much as sending cards that have an irreverent theme. Sometimes sending Groundhog Day cards to your volunteers will show that you have a silly side and they will enjoy it. Slapstick silliness will not fit in your setting, but a little fun will fit even in the most buttoned-up setting. Many people think of inappropriate humor or loud behavior as having fun, but this is not what we are talking about. Beating people down so that someone else feels good is not funny. We are talking about the ability to simply have a belly laugh in the workplace and it's really okay.

Simply showing up for a meeting with a birthday cake or a plate of muffins can lighten up the event. It does not require money to make a lighter setting. Decorating the bosses office just uses creativity. Trips after a tough volunteer assignment to a pizza place for pizza and beer doesn't mean the agency must pay for it. Getting silly after working on an all-nighter can simply give the team a coming together, and build team spirit. Stopping during a particularly difficult period of serious work to play a game of volleyball can do wonders for the volunteer spirit. Stuff and money can help and we will talk later about getting your local vendors to help, but the reality is that everyone can have fun without having stuff.

We have loads of outstanding corporate models to follow, from Apple Computer and Microsoft, to Southwest Airlines, Ben & Jerry's, and Starbucks. These companies exhibit what Dave Hemsath and Leslie Yerkes say in *301 Ways To Have Fun At Work*. It is that "fun at work may be the single most important trait of a highly effective and successful organization."[20] They say that they have seen a direct link between fun at work and employee creativity, productivity, morale, satisfaction, and retention, as well as customer service and many other factors that determine business success.

Fun builds a team spirit as people enjoy having a relaxed and sometimes crazy moment with each other. David Thielen discussing life at Microsoft says, "A cold, sterile, humorless workplace can never develop espirit de corps." He tells a story about a day at Microsoft when one team member went on vacation and that same afternoon everyone else received their first copy of a new software program. To Microsoft members, that is the same as going to Mecca. This poor person on vacation did not get his, so the other team members all put their empty boxes from the software package in his office. His office was filled almost to the ceiling with empty boxes. The authors tell us he was pleased to no end!

Watching a nerf ball being tossed against the wall in the Microsoft halls might seem quite childlike and a waste of company time. But when it's okay to have a blast at work it shows employees that the organization is supportive of them enjoying themselves in the workplace. Southwest Airlines is that kind of place, a fun place, both for customers and for employees. It really all starts at the top, with CEO Herb Kelleher. Kelleher says that anybody who likes to be called a 'professional' probably shouldn't be around Southwest Airlines. He explains that they want people who can do things well with laughter and grace. Herb explains that the professionals that you find at Southwest are people who believe that the business of business is to make a profit by serving people and making life more fun. There are hundreds of Southwest stories, even management guru Tom Peters liked to bring clients to observe Southwest because it was just a fun place to learn how to have fun. Tom Peters, writing the Foreword for Kevin and Jackie Freiberg's book, *Nuts!* Asks, "how has Southwest done all this?" "It's not rocket science...being crazy enough to follow an unorthodox vision, being courageous enough to allow people to have fun and be 'real' people at work, and being smart enough to recognize that their most valuable assets are the people and culture they create. Southwest never forgets it is in the people business—the company just happens to operate an airline."[21]

Anne Bruce and James Pepitone, in their book, *Motivating Employees,* give an example of the level of fun that Southwest employees inflict upon those paying passengers. Here's a rendition of the Southwest flight attendant safety message. "As the song goes, there might be 50 ways to leave your lover, but there are only six ways to leave this aircraft." Followed by, "In the event of a water evacuation, your bottom—your seat bottom, that is—can be used as a flotation device." Then, "Although we never anticipate a change in cabin pressure, should one occur…stop screaming, deposit a quarter, and unlike President Clinton, inhale!"[22] By the time this short message is delivered, the entire plane is laughing and starts to talk with each other.

Having fun at work is all about taking life less seriously. Volunteers function in organizations where serious activity is an every moment event. We have volunteers in spousal abuse centers, working phones on the crisis hot line, in a hospice, or in a hospital. Stress goes with the territory, as does tension. Laughter that comes from the belly helps to break that stress and tension as well as build confidence and make life a little easier overall. Norman Cousins, author of *Anatomy of an Illness*, referred to laughter as one of the healing powers of nature. We are told that laughter, fun, and play are unadult, unintelligent, and nonprofessional. Nothing could be further from the truth. One of the first indicators of the onset of most mental illness is a loss of the sense of joy in being alive.

Many volunteers will move on when their volunteering stops being fun. Remember that before your volunteers will lighten up, you need to lighten up yourself. The attitude of the manager sets the stage for the work environment. Lee Iacoca said, "The speed of the boss is the speed of the team." Maybe we should also say that the laughter of the boss is the laughter of the team. Fun should just happen, it should be spontaneous. The manager does not need to plan fun activities; they just need to allow them to occur. While it's true we need a professional setting to work in, holding in our laughter is not the best guide. Sometimes, having a party or picnic for no reason at all is good therapy for a stressful day. Schedule a volunteer meeting in a more fun place, maybe the local pizza place. Herb Kelleher, the CEO of Southwest Airlines, gives it to us straight, "There's no reason that work has to be suffused with seriousness...Professionalism can be worn lightly. Fun is a stimulant to people. They enjoy their work more and work more productively."

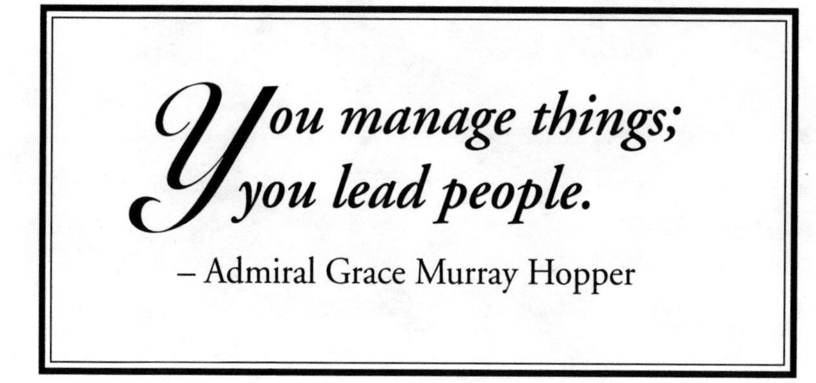
You manage things;
you lead people.
– Admiral Grace Murray Hopper

Chapter Eight

Build Leaders

The one piece of advice which, I believe, will contribute more to making you a better leader is that you must care.

– Lieutenant General Melvin Zais

Leadership is not an inborn trait, leaders are not born with unique leadership abilities, and leaders learn to be leaders. It is a series of tools that one can develop through reading, observing, and practicing. Everyone needs to study leadership. Leadership is different from management. Much of what the volunteer coordinator does is day-to-day management. Warren Bennis, an author who has written a number of classic texts on leadership says, "Leaders are the ones with vision, who inspire others and cause them to galvanize their efforts and achieve change. Managers, on the other hand, will follow standard operating procedure to the grave." Strong? Yes, but to the point. We need to be leaders among our volunteers, and we need to start developing fellow leaders among our troops. In fact, we have a responsibility to develop leadership in others. But how do we do this development and exactly whom should we be developing? Well, according to Patrick Townsend and Joan Gebhardt, in

Five Star Leadership, "...leadership skills must be mastered by everyone in the organization if the organization is to survive."[23]

We should take a few minutes to understand a few differences between leadership and management. These suggestions come from Bennis in his book, *Managing People Is Like Herding Cats.*[24]

1. **The manager maintains; the leader develops.** We have all worked for, or at least observed, people who never want to embrace change, if it's not broken, don't fix it type of attitude. They like the day-to-day to be smooth, no change please. Leaders are always reading about what others are doing. They are going to visit other programs they have heard about. They are attending conferences and spending hours talking to other attendees to gather new ideas.

2. **The manager has his or her eye on the bottom line; the leader has his or her eye on the horizon.** The manager never has enough money to develop recognition programs. They are afraid to speak to the board about major changes in the program because they might require a little money. The leader is out in the community rounding up support for new ways to acknowledge volunteers. They are talking at all the service clubs in town to gather corporate sponsorship for their next dream.

3. **Managers do the things right; leaders do the right things.** This reflects what Stephen Covey meant when he talked about doing first things first. It's the ability that a leader has to set priorities and decide what is truly worth spending time on. Managers, at times, will work on one project after another, never considering which will make a difference and which can afford to wait. Townsend goes a step further when he says, "...managers care that a job gets done, leaders care that a job gets done—and they openly care about the people doing the job."

Both Bennis and Townsend quote Field Marshal Sir William Slim, who led the 14th British Army from 1943 to 1945, who describes this difference between management and leadership. "Managers are necessary; leaders are essential. Leadership is of the spirit, compounded of personality and vision. Management is of the mind, more a matter of accurate calculation, statistics, methods, timetables, and routine." Don't misunderstand all this communication. Managers are very necessary and perform a needed task. We all have days when we should be wearing the manager's hat. Many duties that we take on require this numbers mentality. But unless we exercise our leadership abilities, the volunteer program will stagnate. Leadership is about growth, development, and change. Leadership is about getting our volunteers to take on new roles, to accept a challenge. Leaders are concerned with their guiding purpose, their overarching vision. Bennis says it best, "Leaders have a clear idea of what they want to do...they know where they are going and why."

But just as we need to continually develop our leadership abilities, so do our volunteer leaders need on-going leadership development. One development technique that works well in the corporate arena is cross-functional experience. Letting the volunteer leader get their feet wet in a number of areas. One year the volunteers take on the black tie dinner and the next year they are in charge of planning the reorganization of the gift shop management team. The more they work around the place, the more experience they gather. Working for fellow leaders helps to grow their experience base. Even working for poor leaders helps. They can learn as much, maybe more, from working with poor bosses as good bosses. The difference is that bad bosses teach you what not to do. Bennis gives us advice, maybe with a little humor intended, "The ideal boss for a growing leader is probably a good boss with major flaws, so that one can learn all the complex lessons of what to do and what not to do simultaneously."

If we have the duty to grow our volunteers in leadership, just what does that require? What do the volunteers need to know? Who should we select to develop as leaders? While we could be nice and say that everyone would gain from leadership training, which is true, it is also silly to build all leaders and no workers. We need lots of hard working volunteers to get the day-to-day work done. But we also need a group of people who the volunteers will enjoy being with as their leaders. John Maxwell, in his book *Developing The Leaders Around You,* says this about the development of leaders: "Systems become dated. Buildings deteriorate. Machinery wears. But people can grow, develop, and become more effective if they have a leader who understands their potential value."[25] Maybe Coach John Wooden from UCLA knew the answer best. He said that if you want to develop leaders, you are responsible to appreciate your people for who they are; and then believe that they will do their best. Maxwell says, "Great leaders…all have one thing in common. They know that acquiring and keeping good people is a leader's most important task."

To accomplish that task that your organization has as its driving passion, to change the world, to feed the hungry, to protect the citizens, you must develop leaders around you. You cannot do it all yourself. You must grow leaders. But what do you look for in those potential leaders? Maxwell spells out these qualities; character, influence, a positive attitude, excellent people skills, confidence, self-discipline, effective communication skills, being discontent with the status quo, and a proven track record.

Character: People will only follow others who "walk their talk," who do what they say they are going to do. We have all worked for bosses who would lecture on a topic and live their lives very differently. We lost our belief in this person and thought of them as a manager but not a leader.

Influence: Leadership is really nothing more at times than the ability to influence people to do something. Think about who has influenced you so far in your life. Who are your heroes? Which teachers had the greatest influence over your decisions? Was it your mom or dad that influenced you toward a career? Some people in your life were positional leaders, people who were in a position of power over people but who lacked the ability to lead. We may do the job but we never really hop on the team wagon. They lack the influence over us that creates the passion and drive to move forward. It's the influential leader who fires our soul and creates the excitement to get the job done.

Positive attitude: People do not like working with people who are always grumps. Some people are like Ziggy, always in the dumps. Everything is wrong and there is a dark cloud over their heads! Everybody knows somebody like that and will usually avoid being around that person. The really exciting thing about a positive leader is that they attract others just like them. John Maxwell calls this the law of magnetism.

People skills: People who are leaders like people, they take the time to get to know the people they work with everyday. Being around your people is important, following the "manage by wandering around" technique, but changing into "leading by being with your people." Leaders take the time to talk personally with their team members, not only about the job but more so about life. They stay focused and give "spur of the moment" praisings as a tool to continue the spirit of the workplace.

Confidence: The leader knows they can make it happen. They have both the ability and the confidence to get the job done and as a leader this rubs off on their team. Today we tend to call this passion and it's a good term for this leadership trait. The leader who exhibits excitement, who is passion-filled about a cause, will impact others. People like to follow a winner. It's always amazed me how fast people drift away from last year's ball team if they start losing and lose their confidence in themselves.

Self-discipline: Leaders are willing to stay the course, they will not turn around when the seas are rough. They have a "stick to it" trait that means they finish what they start. They are not afraid to fail and if they do fall down, they get back up and try again. They stay focused on the results they are seeking, that's why other volunteers want to go with them. If something goes wrong they don't look for others to blame, they take the blame. Your people know that if something goes wrong, the leader will not try to pass the buck. They have the Truman attitude of "the buck stops here."

Effective communication skills: The leader knows that to be effective, they must get their message across to everybody.

If they speak at too academic a level they lose some people. If they speak at too elementary a level to others, they get turned off. Communication is a learned skill and one worth a leader's time in learning.

Leaders must be "hands on," out there talking to their people at all times. The message that the leader delivers must always be clear and never fuzzy. Leaders don't talk in jargon. When your people leave a meeting they must understand what was said. Leaders know that long meetings are a waste of time, that meetings must communicate and no more.

Discontent with the status quo: This is just a fancy way of saying that the leader gets bored easily. They want a challenge, and when things are going smoothly, the leader thinks something is wrong. This will frustrate some folks who think we finally got it all working. The leader knows that change is healthy for an organization and works to create this change on a daily basis. They don't "throw out the baby with the bath water." If something is working, maybe a slight change will improve the process.

Proven track record: The world loves organizations that are consistent, that keep on going. It's like the Energizer bunny commercials, where the batteries don't fail and the bunny keeps going, and going, and going. People also like leaders who are consistent, who don't bend in the wind. People don't automatically follow people because they are elected or have a title. They watch to see if leaders conduct their private lives in concert with their stated objectives, in other words, do they "walk their talk?"

Finding potential leaders requires work on your part. It requires going through your inventory of volunteer help and doing a quiet analysis of each person's abilities and performance record. Leadership is learned. You are not born a leader, you develop the skills a little at a time. To develop leaders you must have training and patience, they are not grown in a day. You select people with leadership potential and then help them grow themselves into leaders. Two of the best books to use in developing leadership training is Rick Pitino's *Lead To Succeed* which outlines the 10 traits of leadership, and John Maxwell's *The 21 Indispensable Qualities of a Leader.*

Your job as a leader, developing your fellow leaders is to develop a climate within your organization that makes it possible for people to succeed. It is truly the attitude of the leader that creates the climate that allows people to accomplish great things. Never give up on your people and build failure into your system. Letting people fail and then helping them learn from it is a critical step in the development of leadership. But the leader has to illustrate that everyday. Great performance by a volunteer is a journey, not a destination. Everyone learns by doing. It takes time and practice, as well as some failure. Don Shula, when he was coach of the Miami Dolphins said, "Success is not forever, and failure isn't fatal." This suggests that we need to keep things in perspective. And lastly, try to follow Ken Blanchard's advice from his book, *Leadership and the One Minute Manager*, "Leadership is not something you do to people. It's something you do with people."[26]

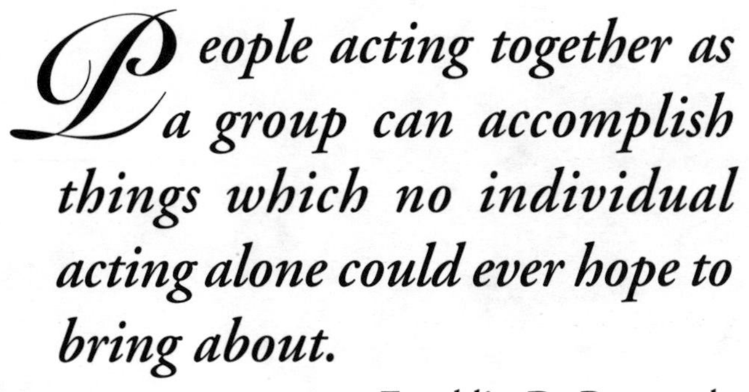
People acting together as a group can accomplish things which no individual acting alone could ever hope to bring about.
– Franklin D. Roosevelt

Chapter Nine

Build That Team!

When you're hiring, you want people who love you and love the values of your company. You don't want confrontation all the time. Also you don't want people who have only a sense of their own growth, not that of others, or of the company's.

– Anita Roddick, The Body Shop

Pat Williams, in his book *The Magic of Teamwork* says, "Simply stated, a team attitude is a 'we' and 'our' attitude instead of a 'me' and 'my' attitude."[27] Pat worked for years as the executive vice president of the Orlando Magic basketball team and he knows what he is talking about. When volunteers start working together as a team, rather than as individuals, they can accomplish so much more. There is a synergy or flow that occurs as people come together to perform a task as a group. But how do you get it started, how do you build individuals into a cohesive working team? Peter Senge, author of *The Fifth Discipline*, offers this observation, "When a team becomes more aligned, a commonality of direction emerges and individual energies harmonize. There is less wasted energy. In fact, a resonance or synergy develops like the coherent light of a laser rather than the incoherent and scattered light of a light bulb. There is a commonality of purpose, a shared vision, an understanding of how to complement one another's efforts."[28]

In sports, being a team member and fighting for a team win is an important concept. We can do the same thing in the volunteer environment; we can carry this excitement and desire to make a difference into the volunteer setting. We can get the volunteers serving on a team where they complement and support each other in a way that improves the organization. We need to start our team building with clarity of purpose and strong direction. It starts with a true north, knowing exactly what our direction is, where we, as a group or team, are heading. What are we trying to accomplish as an organization? You cannot get the whole group behind the effort unless everyone understands the purpose and everyone knows how to get there. Karl Albrecht uses the metaphor of riding a train in his book, *The Northbound Train*, as he talks about the idea of creating the vision and meaning that allows an organization to move forward. Albrecht says, "It is the leader who must choose the train, as a matter of careful thinking and strategy formulation. The leader must help people in the organization understand and commit to the vision. And the leader must help them learn to do what it takes to make the vision a reality."[29]

Knowing where the organization is going, or where they should be heading, is critical to its success as a team. How do we create this direction or vision for our team? Part of this vision originates with the leader, the executive director, in agreement with the organization's board. The overall direction for the organization must always come from the top, from the leadership. But before the organization can move forward with a strong sense of purpose, the team itself must buy into the dream. The team must accept and incorporate the vision. But before we can ask the team to buy into that dream, we as leaders must distill the vision down to its essential elements, the core of the vision.

Exactly what are we trying to accomplish as an organization? Why is this dream important? What will accomplishing this dream do for people? As a leadership team, we must first put these thoughts down in clear black and white. We must have a clear understanding of the purpose that we pursue. This must include knowing what we are working at today and where we are heading tomorrow. Knowing our purpose and seeing our future must be stated in our mission statement. The volunteer coordinator usually has little to do with the overall agency mission statement. It was set, probably years ago, by the board and the top supporters of the organization. But each volunteer component of the organization needs their own direction; they need their own sense of direction, their own mission statement. This mission statement must be simple, clear, common sense, and easy to apply in the volunteer setting. It needs to be developed through a groupthink process, formulated as a result of volunteer brainstorming sessions. The mission statement must reflect the attitudes and feelings of the volunteers on the team. It must be their feelings that are reflected in their mission statement. It is a good idea to revisit that mission statement every year to allow the team to rethink their vision.

Habitat for Humanity is an excellent example of an organization that knows exactly who they are and where they are going. Their mission statement is "to eliminate poverty housing from the world and to make decent shelter a matter of conscience and action." This is clear to both those who volunteer and to those companies who give funds to Habitat. They realize that volunteers are the key to their success in meeting their goals and they allow volunteers to serve in leadership roles in further developing their vision.

Many times the organization is unsure what they expect their volunteers to accomplish. They either expect too much from their volunteers or they seem to lack respect for the quality of volunteer work. The volunteer mission statement needs to reflect the organization's attitude toward their volunteer base. Does the organization see volunteers as an important core element? Do they plan to let the volunteers run their place, or are volunteers simply worker-bees to be directed and thanked? This statement must establish the value of volunteers in the overall agency mission plan. The volunteers themselves, with the assistance of the volunteer director and the other agency leaders, must generate the mission statement for the volunteer program. The mission statement must be the result of many hours of brainstorming and groupthink activities. It needs to be passed around, commented on and allowed to transform through individual comments. This process of growing a sense of volunteer mission is itself a very important team-building process. It is a form of coming together, which will build team spirit and attitude. Be sure you involve as many people in the process as you can. But you must also be willing to call a halt at the right time. Work needs to be done if you are going to get underway in doing the real work that the volunteers are there to accomplish. When you have a high degree of agreement on a statement of purpose, stop the process and celebrate. It is a good idea to hold a party and present the overall statement that will hang on the wall and be a part of the new volunteer handbook.

Bob Nelson, in his book, *1001 Ways To Energize Employees*, discusses how managers can energize their teams by communicating their personal vision of what teamwork means to them. He illustrates his point by showing how Nancy Singer, from First of America Bank Corporation, gets it done. Nancy bought computer mouse pads and note cubes for her teams and inscribed them with the word teamwork. Nancy put this acronym for teamwork on the pads and cubes:

Together

Everyone

Achieves

More

With

Organization

Recognition and

Knowledge[30]

The team that makes the most mistakes will probably win. The doer makes mistakes, and I want doers on my team, players who make things happen.

– John Wooden

Chapter Ten

They call it coaching, but it is teaching.
You do not tell them it is so.
You show them it is so.

– Vince Lombardi

What is a coach? To me, a coach is one who gives praise when the volunteer has earned it, and helps them improve their performance when it is needed. Coaches are folks who can motivate, teach, reward, and discipline. They are people who can transfer knowledge from one head to another, to help people become the best they can be at the task before them. NFL coaching legend Don Shula says a coach's job is "to instruct, discipline, and inspire them to do things better than they thought they could do them on their own."[31] Shula states that the real work performed by the coach "comes down to a matter of motivating people to work hard and prepare to play as a team. That's what really counts. In a word, it's coaching." In other words, the coach has the job of preparing people to perform at the best of their ability.

We have to understand that every organization is either continuing to improve or it's getting worse. We must be always learning and improving what we do. It is the coach that guides this constant improvement. The coach models the commitment to constant improvement. Coaching involves a series of conversations that the volunteer coordinator has with her players, her team members. A good definition of coaching is that it is an activity that improves performance which leads to the volunteer doing an excellent job. The American Society for Training and Development (ASTD) defines coaching as an activity that leads to the continuous improvement of performance.[32] They state that coaching requires a conversation that involves at least two people. This must be a conversation that results in the improvement of performance. This activity should be results-oriented, in other words, it leads to an improved level of activity. It may involve a conversation with a volunteer working in the gift store where you give suggestions for improving their sales techniques. You are not being critical of what they are doing. In fact, you have praised their friendliness and customer service. You are suggesting new techniques for adding to each buyer's purchase amount, something they call up-selling. You give a few techniques and then leave a short book on the topic with the volunteer.

Coaches believe that people want to improve their performance, and they must be given the opportunity to demonstrate their competence. They also believe that people are not guided by control but by the freedom to do the job themselves in their own way and at their speed. To perform at this peak level, your people must understand the work is important and they must know how to perform the task at hand. The coach must express his or her expectations of the volunteer and must give appreciation for the task when completed.

Many volunteers feel that they have ideas and suggestions for improving the workflow in the agency, but they are not sure that anyone wants to hear their thoughts. Do your volunteers feel comfortable coming to you with their suggestions? Are you open to hearing them? Do you make the time to sit down with your team members on a daily basis? Marshall Cook, in his book *Effective Coaching,* gives us an excellent "Accessibility Quotient" quiz. He asks how your workers would respond to the following statements. He asks you to think about how your team members would respond.

My director,

1. Asks for my opinion frequently.
2. Listens to my suggestions.
3. Takes my ideas seriously.
4. Values my opinion.
5. Checks with me before making a decision that affects my work.
6. Explains goals clearly when giving me a new project.

7. Welcomes my questions about an ongoing project.
8. Gives me latitude in deciding how to carry out a project.
9. Saves criticism for one-on-one sessions.[33]

How did you do when you answered these questions yourself? One of the goals of becoming a strong coach is to create an environment where the volunteer coordinator and the volunteer can sit down together and discuss things. Volunteers all arrive at the volunteer place wanting to do an outstanding job. But all of us make mistakes and need constant reinforcement in the workplace. It is the volunteer coordinator, wearing the coaching cap, that has the opportunity to make or break the new volunteer.

We have been discussing the volunteer director's ability to listen to the volunteers. People respect people who are willing to hear them out. When a volunteer makes a mistake, the first thing to do is to listen to them. Ask why they did it that way, but be open to listening to their response. Do not assume that you know why they performed that way before they answer. Assumptions are always dangerous, and quite often wrong. Listening is one of the keys to success. We need to hear more than what the other person is saying. Real listening means giving them your full and undivided attention. Sometimes that means putting aside more important things to listen to the volunteer. Sometimes it means finding quiet space out of the office to sit down with the volunteer. Listening to your team member is showing them trust and caring.

When your volunteers know that you are willing to listen to them, they will come to you more often to talk about issues that concern them. As a university professor, I found that by showing up a little early before class and staying a few minutes after class, I had a few students who would drop in to talk. By listening to them talk about their home life or work life, I started to sense why they were having problems in class. Everything in one's life is connected. Your volunteer, who is so unconnected and scattered, may be going through a divorce or has a sick child to contend with at home. By spending a few minutes in conversation, you are coaching this person by listening to them. Remember that the person's voice, choice of words, speed of talking and body language may all give you clues to what is really going on.

Part of our listening skills is really relating skills. Ian Mackay, in his book *Listening Skills,* gives us suggestions for improving our listening abilities. Mackay says, "Attending physically involves you, as the listener, adopting an attitude of involvement: showing the speaker that you are 'with' them just by your physical attitude or posture."[34] Have you ever been talking with your boss at a cocktail reception and noticed that the boss was spending most of his concentration searching the room for someone more important to talk to than you? It is very frustrating to attempt a conversation with someone who is "not there." They are so distracted that it's not worth the attempt. Mackay suggests that the four key steps to attending physically is to face the speaker directly, maintain good eye contact, maintain an open posture, and remain relaxed. You need to let people know that you are listening and attending in a psychological way as well. This involves your concentrating on the person you are listening to by focusing on what is being said and even how it is being said. It is difficult at times to listen to what is not being said and to gauge the feelings that are being expressed. Sometimes the person speaking shows anger or uses emotion-laden terms that will cause you to miss the real point. This is the time to relax, give the issue focus and try to see where the person is coming from. One of my most difficult habits is the desire to interrupt the speaker early in the conversation and interject my opinions. I want to say something. But it is not time yet, the other person has the floor and needs to fully express their thoughts first. If we spend our listening time composing our comeback statement or, even worse, our 'yes, but' statement, we will find it is hard to stay active in our listening. Active listening may be an overused term but it does have relevance here. To remain active means to hold that eye contact, nod your head to indicate listening, maybe ask a question, and restate what the other person has said to create understanding. Mackay gives the characteristics of the ideal listener that he gathered from a research study at Ohio State University. The ideal listener:

> Primarily keeps an open, curious mind. He listens for new ideas everywhere, integrating what he hears with what he already knows.

> He is also self-perceptive and listens to others with his total being. Thus he becomes personally involved with what he hears...He looks for ideas, organization and arguments but always listens to the essence of things. Knowing that no two people listen the same, he stays mentally alert...He is introspective but has the capacity and desire to critically examine, understand and attempt to transform some of his values, attitudes and relationships within himself and with others. He focuses his mind on the listening and listens to the speaker's ideas, but he also listens with feelings and intuition.

Coaching is hard work. It requires you to involve yourself with your team. You cannot sit on the sidelines and watch your team, it's time to get involved. Frank McNair, in his book *It's OK to Ask 'Em to Work,* quotes coach Bear Bryant who reduced all coaching to five steps.

1. Tell the team players what you expect from them.
2. Give them the opportunity to perform.
3. Give them feedback about how they are doing.
4. Coach with suggestions for improvement when needed. And,
5. Reward them on a regular basis for the contribution they made.[35]

I think you will agree with me that Coach Bryant hits the nail on the head. He had defined the day-to-day job of the volunteer coordinator in very common sense terms that we can apply everyday.

Keep away from people who try to belittle your ambitions. Small people always do that, but the really great make you feel that you too, can become great.

– Mark Twain

Chapter Eleven

Build Motivation

Flatter me, and I may not believe you.
Criticize me, and I may not like you.
Ignore me, and I may not forgive you.
Encourage me, and I will not forget you.

– William Arthur Ward

If you walk through your local Barnes & Noble superstore you will find rows of books devoted to motivating people. You will find out how to motivate employees, teenagers, your spouse, and even yourself. Motivation will discuss getting your own attitude straight and firing up your passion for the work you do and the life you lead. Motivation seems to be a key word in today's environment from Amway to Starbucks. But just what is motivation and how do we do it? Our approach will involve setting a work environment that will allow volunteers to rediscover their hidden self-motivation and thereby help the entire team to grow in motivation.

Motivation comes in two forms, high and low. Those volunteers who are in a state of excitement and have a daily readiness to get the job done are known as passionate, highly motivated volunteers. Just give them the work and get out of their way. Other volunteers seem to be in a state of demotivation, they have low productivity, high absenteeism and negative attitudes, and spend much of their time complaining about the tasks at hand. It seems that as volunteer coordinators get together and talk about their workdays, it is the "lack of motivation" that is the topic of conversation. In Dennis Waitley's book, *The Psychology of Winning*, Waitley discusses that a lack of motivation is one of the most troublesome problems managers face.[36] Nothing is more frustrating than to walk around a volunteer place and see volunteers with low energy levels, waiting to be told what to do, showing low initiative and offering poor customer service.

What is it that gets some volunteers up and running at full speed and holds back others, keeping them in a negative mood? Dean Spitzer in his book, *SuperMotivation*, says that every worker needs ability plus high motivation.[37] Think about the volunteers who have simply made a difference in the world. The ability comes from an intensive training program, and probably you have that in place already. You fully understand that to have a high performing volunteer requires on-the-job training. If you are hiring new volunteer meals-on-wheels drivers, you are going to schedule a few days of training. You will train them in health and safety and protecting the food that they will deliver from spoilage. You will train them in safe driving techniques and map reading skills. You will talk at length about the clients they will see daily, the older seniors who are shut-ins. All of this training though, will not have anything to do with motivation. In fact, the truth is, you cannot really do anything to motivate other people. You can only influence what they're motivated to do. People really have to motivate themselves. Volunteer managers will influence the volunteer's motivation every time they arrive for their assignment. And you can either motivate or demotivate that volunteer.

Anne Bruce and James Pepitone in their book, *Motivating Employees*, tell us, "Motivation…is intrinsic—it's inside us." This means that we experience what is in the world around us and react to it. Something will make us feel good and something else will bother us. Some people will turn us on and others will shut us down. It's not really the people that cause that, it's what those people do or say to us that motivates or demotivates us. Sometimes the motivation is extrinsic, meaning it's outward recognition, prizes won for sales contests, our picture in the newspaper. But even these extrinsic motivators will have a lot to do with our innermost feeling of self worth and future goals. Many people feel that these extrinsic rewards are motivating factors, but before they can serve as a motivator, we must accept them, we must buy in to them as motivators. Isn't it possible for someone to give us a gift and we might assume that the person wants something from us, and then the gift becomes demotivating? We must see a connection between the gift and the reason that it was given to us.

Volunteer expectations are critical to the volunteer's motivations. What the volunteer expects to receive from their volunteering will show us what the driving force is inside the volunteer. It's a case of asking what the volunteer feels is in it for them. It's the positive side of the question, "What's in it for me?" To help the manager motivate the volunteer they must uncover the volunteer's reasons for doing things. If the volunteer expects to meet a lot of nice people to socialize with and finds that nobody introduces them around and, in fact, the job they are given has no social contact, they will be demotivated. A well planned and delivered orientation can give the volunteer the correct expectations. If the volunteer knows what to expect and the organization delivers those expectations, it's a win-win situation.

Motivation cannot be a quick fix, nor can it be a one kind fits all approach. Too many organizations have had the "program of the month" type of volunteer motivation program. It isn't that these programs don't work; it's just that any one program isn't going to work for all volunteers. Everyone is motivated by something or somebody, but it may not be you, or your agency, or the work you have assigned to that volunteer. You have seen demotivated workers who, at 5 pm, jump up and literally run to the cocktail lounge or basketball court. They are certainly motivated then! We also make the mistake that giving the volunteers physical rewards will always motivate them. Physical rewards, like certificates, t-shirts, etc. do not guarantee a long-term motivational strategy. Depending upon the criteria for presenting these rewards, they may be honoring the wrong thing. They may be sending the message that loyalty is more important than excellence. Giving awards based on the number of hours a volunteer gives to the agency will emphasize loyalty and fail to reinforce the quality of volunteer performance. It may be better to acknowledge the increased positive comment cards generated by the senior citizens following the presentations at the senior center by a volunteer.

Motivating today's new volunteer requires a new form of motivation. Today's volunteer expects to be involved in the organization, to have a say in the planning of activities. They expect to be assigned enjoyable, stimulating, and challenging work. It must be work that has meaning and they personally must understand the meaning of the work. They want rewards and recognition that is based on their own outstanding performance, rather than for the mere fact that they have been showing up at the volunteer place. We have a different volunteer today, more ethnic diversity, a much higher proportion of male volunteers, and a larger number that are from nontraditional family backgrounds. These differences make it much more difficult for any "cookie cutter" type of motivation to work.

The best motivation comes from within us. It is not chasing the carrot that truly motivates us. It is not the rewards and the praise that really motivate us; it is our desire for something. Waitley has stated, "For too long…it has been wrongly assumed that motivation…can be pumped in from the outside through incentives, pep talks, contests, rallies, and sermons." In fact, too many outside rewards will cause the loss of self-motivation, the driving force of the volunteer getting the work done. Spitzer says, "If high performance is going to be sustained, motivation must ultimately come from the inside out, rather than the outside in."

Motivation is really a form of energy, it is the passion exhibited by the excited volunteer. This passion is what pushes us forward; it's what will release all that energy that makes us take on those volunteer assignments. It's what gives us the energy to work for months on a fund-raising project or building a house for Habitat. The traditional theories on motivation suggest that we are motivated by needs. You know, as in Maslow, we are motivated by need reduction, we need food and water, and then we have social needs. Most of us have little problem meeting our food and water needs, but much trouble with these social needs. Spitzer defines these needs as "things we actively want; they might make us happier and more effective, but we will not die without them. When we desire something strongly enough, we become very persistent in its pursuit." His book, *SuperMotivation,* gives us the eight human desires, each of which he says gives us the potential for releasing enormous amounts of motivational energy. These desires are for activity, ownership, power, affiliation, competence, achievement, recognition, and meaning. We should all recognize these as exactly those needs that volunteers express on a daily basis. Let's look at how our volunteers express these desires.

The desire for activity, which reflects the innate human orientation toward stimulation—to be active, to be engaged, and to enjoy life. All volunteers come aboard looking for work that needs to be done. They find personal motivation by being involved in activities that are stimulating. The desire for ownership, which reflects the fact that volunteers want to "own their work"; in fact they would like significant input into their work. The volunteer program should belong to the volunteers. They should be in leadership positions where they are making decisions as well as making a difference. The desire for power is important and we tend to use empowerment as a management tool since it tends to allow volunteers to make their own decisions in the workplace. Try to put your volunteers into positions where they can empower others. The desire for affiliation comes from our strong human need to socialize with each other. The volunteer setting allows the volunteer to meet new people and to develop meaningful relationships. Affiliation is one of the primary motivators for volunteers and one that you need to satisfy to retain the volunteer. The desire for competence requires continual learning, and the volunteer setting fosters new learning through training sessions that are ongoing. Volunteer places need to be learning organizations. Training is an ongoing, everyday activity. The desire for achievement has a lot to do with the feeling of succeeding. All volunteers want to have the feeling that they are accomplishing something worthwhile, that they are doing it themselves. Volunteers need to feel that the work they are doing has a strong purpose. The desire for recognition means that everyone wants to feel appreciated by others. This can be in private or in a public setting, but it is the desire that motivates them. The desire for meaning is critical to all volunteers. Every volunteer wants to feel that they are making a difference in someone's life through the work that they are doing. Meaningful work is the number one motivator for all volunteers.

You may be the most capable manager in the volunteer world, but unless your volunteers are highly motivated, you will be working alone. These desires are one of the major keys to volunteer retention. I think you can see how each volunteer is driven by a different combination of these desires. It's also why the volunteer coordinator goes home tired at night attempting to meet all of their volunteers' expectations and individual desires.

Any fact facing us is not as important as our attitude toward it, for that determines our success or failure.

– Norman Vincent Peale

Chapter Twelve

Look for Attitude

You are the way you are because that's the way you wanted to be. If you really wanted to be any different, you would be in the process of changing right now.

– Fred Smith, FedEx

People with positive attitudes are fun people to be around. For them, every cloud has a silver lining and rain showers will bring rainbows to enjoy. People with negative attitudes see rain as a potential thunderstorm, and trouble brewing ahead. Attitude is a direction, either toward success or failure. We cannot always control how things go, but we can control our attitude toward the things that happen. Some people are fun to be around and some people are a pain. Burke Hedges, in his book *You, Inc.* states it best; "Everybody lights up a room. Some when they enter…some when they leave."[38] We want volunteers who light up our place when they enter!

How many times have you had to work with a negative volunteer? I had Fred at the front desk in the City Hall. He was always unfriendly and often nasty to the guests who walked into the City Hall. He would answer their questions with a short reply and a growl, never with a smile. I wondered why he was always in a bad mood. Nothing I did or said to Fred seemed to make him get any better. I finally reassigned him to work alone in the back room and away from other people. He was a great computer engineer and he did build a fantastic database for us, but nothing ever made him smile. The real issue with these negative people is that their negativity rubs off on strong positive volunteers. My wife Ann had a friend like Fred. Whenever Ann went to visit her friend, she would come home in a fairly negative mood herself and was unable to figure out what had happened. She would leave the house bright and happy, and one hour later it was gone.

The truth is that we choose to see the future, either through rose colored glasses or dark glasses. It's our attitudes that differ, not reality. Some people grumble about everything, nothing is ever okay. When the new volunteer comes in with a negative attitude, it makes it difficult to start the relationship. We want good working relationships between the people who work at our place and negative people are hard to work with. I once had a volunteer that nobody wanted to work with; nobody wanted her on his or her team. She ended up being moved from place to place. I wondered why. When I had the opportunity to sit down with this volunteer over a cup of coffee, I saw it immediately. Everything was a problem (from the first words out of her mouth to the last!). She was very negative about everything and everybody. Even I wanted to finish my coffee and get back to work and away from her. She was a wonderful person with a bad attitude.

What is an attitude? It is a set of feelings or beliefs inside you that cause you to view the world as positive or negative. These beliefs and feelings cause you to react to people in certain ways. Your attitude has been shaped by what has happened to you over the years, as well as by the people you associate with. Your attitude has a lot to do with your outward personality. You cannot change someone else's attitude. Only they can change their attitude. Willie Jolley, a motivational speaker from Washington, DC, uses this thought as the cover of his book, *It Only Takes a Minute To Change Your Life.*[39] Willie is right, we can change our attitudes toward anything with the snap of a finger!

I remember about a year ago when my wife and I were fast-food junkies, running through airports grabbing a McDonalds on the run. We never thought about vitamins and our only exercise was that run through the airport trying to catch that late flight. It literally took us only a minute to say STOP. We had attended a presentation at the National Speakers Association convention from a gentleman known as "The Mango Man." He was called that because he gives talks on living a healthy life and he pushed eating fruits and vegetables over a heavy amount of meat products. We listened to his talk and afterwards we talked about what we had heard. That afternoon we changed our life! Now a year later, we eat very little beef, consume loads of fruit and veggies, walk three miles a day and take supplements every morning. The result is we feel wonderful, have both lost weight, my blood pressure has gone way down and this change took about a minute.

What really changed was our attitude toward living in a healthier way. It was a change in our attitude toward life.

Peter Hirsch wrote a book, *Living With Passion,* in which he says, "Attitude is the switch that turns on everything else."[40] That is so true when it comes to the volunteers. The quality of their attitude reflects on their ability to work well with others and how well they perform their tasks. Hirsch also gives insight with the statement that, "People don't care how much you know, until they know how much you care." Don't get me wrong, negative thinking has a place and positive thinking cannot solve the world's problems. Things do go wrong and they will not be fixed with a positive attitude. We need to be realistic about problems. We need to be realistic when we face a problem or a challenge. But negative thinking can lead to your giving up, and that is no solution either. The positive person will accept problems as challenges and start looking for solutions.

The most important thing to consider when selecting a volunteer is their attitude. An interesting model to follow is Southwest Airlines. Anyone who has flown on Southwest will tell you it's a fun experience. The crew works hard at making your flight a fun one. To Southwest fun is about attitude, so Southwest hires for attitude and trains for skills. Their CEO, Herb Kelleher, says, "We look for attitudes; people with a sense of humor who don't take themselves too seriously. We'll train you on whatever it is you have to do, but the one thing Southwest cannot change in people is inherent attitudes." In other words, they look for the right attitude in their people. This is exactly what we need to do when interviewing potential volunteers. Look for people with the right spirit. Even at Southwest, not everyone passes the screening process. Kevin and Jackie Freiberg, in their book *Nuts*, a book about Southwest Airlines, tells a story about a pilot interview. The interview was with a highly decorated military pilot, one who was ranked first on that day's applicants. But the pilot was rude to the customer service agent and even more rude to the receptionist. This rudeness convinced the interview team that even though the pilot was technically qualified, he didn't have the right attitude for Southwest. He was disqualified.

My suggestion is that we learn to follow the same hiring procedure as Southwest. If a potential volunteer has a negative attitude, is rude to any of your people, don't accept them as a volunteer. We need to realize that we have the right to refuse volunteers. We may feel awkward turning down volunteers, but if you accept people with negative attitudes, you are probably going to lose a few outstanding volunteers who get frustrated by your new recruit.

It's important to realize that we, as volunteer coordinators, cannot motivate anyone, we can only create an environment in which the volunteers motivate themselves. In our seminar, I stress the radio station that all volunteers listen to, WII-FM. I tell everyone that WII-FM is the one radio station that broadcasts everywhere and that everyone listens to it.

With a laugh, I tell them the call letters WII-FM stands for What's In It For Me! We question when we take on a volunteer assignment whether it is a good use of our time. It's not as selfish as it sounds. Why do you work where you work? The pay? Benefits? It's close to home? It has a future? Opportunity to network? These are your WII-FM. Your volunteers check their WII-FM before they say yes to accepting a volunteer assignment. They have only so much time for volunteering; they want to insure that your place is a good use of their time. They want to know that your place will make a difference in someone's life.

We need to assign work to our volunteers that lets them chase their passions. Volunteers have spent their work lives chasing money and careers. When they volunteer they select a place where they can make a difference. You will find that when you get the right mix of volunteer and passion, the volunteer lights up. They don't question the length of volunteer hours, they don't even think about recognition. They motivate themselves producing peak performance. This motivation comes from within the volunteer, it's not something we do to them. True, we must treat them right, praise them continuously, and meet their expectations. But the true motivation is within the heart of the volunteer. The late Ray Kroc, founder of McDonalds said that "...most people find it difficult to associate applause with their work when they can't hear literal applause, but the important applause should come from within." [41]

The critical work of the volunteer coordinator is simply selecting the right person and matching them to the right assignment. While it's a simple thought, it requires a lot of effort to interview many volunteers to select the best ones and then it requires an equal effort to find the best assignment for each one. The theme of this book has been to keep those volunteers around, that is retaining the volunteers. I have tried to illustrate how the correct selection process, careful matching of the assignment to the volunteer, building a caring environment that fosters this relationship, and rewarding them continuously is the simple solution. This simple solution will require your total dedication to the task and it will be worth it as you see your volunteers glow with excitement. There is nothing more thrilling than watching a loving volunteer performing at their best. Give it your best effort and you will be rewarded with the best career you will ever have!

Endnotes

1 Robert Wendover. *2 Minute Motivation.* Naperville, IL: Sourcebooks, Inc., 1995.

2 Richard Carlson, *Don't Sweat The Small Stuff...and it's all small stuff,* New York: Hyperion, 1997.

3 Jim Harris, *The Employee Comnnection,* Successories, Inc., 1998.

4 Alice Potter, *Putting the Positive Thinker To Work,* New York: Berkley Books, 1998.

5 Don Blohowiak, *Think Like Einstein, Create Like Da Vinci, and Invent Like Edison,* Burr Ridge,IL: Irwin Professional Publishing, 1995.

6 Robert Heller, *Tom Peters,* New York: Dorling Kindersley Publishing, Inc., 2000.

7 Martin W. Sandler & Deborah A. Hudson, *Beyond The Bottom Line,* New York: Oxford university Press, 1998.

8 James A. Belasco, *Teaching the Elephant To Dance,* New York: A Plume Book, 1991.

9 Kenneth Blanchard & Spencer Johnson, *The One Minute Manager,* New York: Berkley Books, 1982.

10 Rick Pitino, *Lead To Succeed,* New York: Broadway Books, 2000.

11 Lou Holtz, *Winning Every Day,* New York: HarperBusiness, 1998.

12 John C. Maxwell, *The 21 Irrefutable Laws Of Leadership,* Nashville: Thomas Nelson Publishers, 1998.

13 Betsy Sanders, *Fabled Service,* San Diego: Pfeiffer & Company, 1995.

14 Robert Spector, *Lessons From the Nordstrom Way,* New York: John Wiley & Sons, Inc., 2001.

15 David Thielen, *The 12 Simple Secrets of Microsoft Management,* New York: McGraw-Hill, 1999.

16 Zig Ziglar, *Over The Top,* Nashville: Thomas Nelson Publishers, 1994.

17 Tom Peters, *Reinventing Work: The Professional Service Firm,* New York: Alfred A. Knopf, Inc., 1999.

18 Ron Zemke, *Managing Knock Your Socks Off Service,* New York: AMACOM, 1992.

19 Jeffrey Gitomer, *Customer Satisfaction Is Worthless,* Austin, Texas: Bard Press, 1998.

20 Dave Hemsath & Leslie Yerkes, *301 Ways To Have Fun At Work,* San Francisco: Berrett-Koehler Publishers, Inc., 1997.

21 Kevin Freiberg & Jackie Freiberg, *Nuts!* Austin, Texas: Bard Press, 1996.

22 Anne Bruce & James S. Pepitone, *Motivating Employees,* New York: McGraw-Hill, 1999.

23 Patrick L. Townsend & Joan E. Gebhardt, *Five-Star Leadership,* New York: John Wiley & Sons, Inc., 1997.

24 Warren Bennis, *Managing People Is Like Herding Cats,* Provo, Utah: Executive Excellence Publishing, 1997.

25 John Maxwell, *Developing The Leaders Around You,* Nashville: Thomas Nelson Publishers, 1995.

26 Ken Blanchard, *Leadership and the One Minute Manager,* New York: William Morrow & Company, 1985.

27 Pat Williams, *The Magic of Teamwork,* Nashville: Thomas Nelson Publishers, 1997.

28 Peter Senge, *The Fifth Discipline,* New York: Doubleday & Company, 1994.

29 Karl Albrecht, *The Northbound Train,* New York: AMACOM, 1994.

30 Bob Nelson, *1001 Ways To Energize Employees,* New York: Workman Publishing, 1997.

31 Don Shula & Ken Blanchard, *Everyone's A Coach,* New York: HarperBusiness, 1995.

32 Dennis Kinlaw, *Coaching: The ASTD's Sourcebook,* New York: McGraw-Hill, 1996.

33 Marshall J. Cook, *Effective Coaching,* New York: McGraw-Hill,1999.

34 Ian Mackay, *Listening Skills,* London: Institute Of Personnel And Development, 1984.

35 Frank McNair, *It's OK to Ask 'Em to Work,* New York: AMACOM, 2000.

36 Dennis Waitley, *The Psychology of Winning,* New York: Berkley Books, 1984.

37 Dean Spitzer, *Super-Motivation,* New York: AMACOM, 1995.

38 Burke Hedges, *You, Inc.,* Tampa: INTI Publishing, 1996.

39 Willie Jolley, *It Only Takes A Minute To Change Your Life,* New York: St. Martins Press, 1997.

40 Peter Hirsch, *Living With Passion,* Charlottesville, Virginia: MLM Publishing, Inc., 1994.

41 Denis Waitley and Boyd Matheson, *Attitude: Your Internal Compass,* Successories Library, 1997.

Resources

This Resource List includes all those hard to find addresses and phone numbers of organizations, insurance firms, and catalogs. It also has a listing of the outstanding books in the volunteer field and a collection of very helpful websites.

ORGANIZATIONS

American Association For Museum Volunteers
American Association of Museums
1225 I Street NW
Washington, DC 20005
(202) 289-6575

America's Promise – The Alliance for Youth
909 N. Washington Street,
Suite 400
Alexandria, VA 22314
(703) 684-4500
www.americaspromise.org

American Society of Directors of Volunteer Services
PO Box 75315
Chicago, IL 60675
Contact: Tara O'Briskie
312-422-3863

Association for Volunteer Administration (AVA)
PO Box 32092
3108 Parham Road, Suite 200-B
Richmond, VA 23294
(804) 346-2266
Fax (804) 346-3318
avaintl@mindspring.com
www.avaintl.org

Big Brothers Big Sisters of America
230 N. 13th Street
Philadelphia, PA 19107-1538
(215) 567-7000
www.bbbsa.org

Communities In Schools
277 S. Washington Street,
Suite 210
Alexandria, VA 22314
(703) 519-8999
www.cisnet.org

Corporation for National Service
1201 New York Ave., NW
Washington, DC 20525
(202) 606-5000
www.nationalservice.org

Foster Grandparent Program
Corporation for National Service
1201 New York Ave., NW
Washington, DC 20525
(800) 424-8867
www.nationalservice.org

Independent Sector
1200 Eighteenth Street, NW
Washington, DC 20036
(202) 467-6100
Fax (202) 467-6101
Publications (888) 860-8118
info @ IndependentSector.org
www. IndependentSector.org

National Association of Volunteer Programs in Local Government
440 First St NW
Washington, DC 20001
Contact: Dawn Matheny
707-527-2317

National Center for Nonprofit Boards
1828 L Street, NW, Suite 900
Washington, DC 20036
800-883-6262
www.ncnb.org

National Council of Nonprofit Associations
1001 Connecticut Ave, NW, Suite 900
Washington, DC 20036
(202) 833-5740
www.ncna.org

National Youth Leadership Council
1910 West County Road B
Roseville, MN 55113
(612) 631-3672

Nonprofit Risk Management Center
1001 Connecticut Ave NW, Suite 410
Washington, DC 20036
(202) 785-3891
Fax (202) 296-0349
www.nonprofitrisk.org

Points of Light Foundation
1400 I Street, NW, Ste 800
Washington, DC 20005
(800) 272-8306
Fax (703) 803-9291
www.pointsoflight.org

Public Risk Management Association
1815 N. Fort Myer Drive, Suite 1020
Arlington, VA 22209
(703) 528-7701
www.primacentral.org

Retired Senior Volunteer Program (RSVP)
Corporation for National Service
1201 New York Ave., NW
Washington, DC 20525
(800) 424-8867
www.nationalservice.org

Senior Companion Program
Corporation for National Service
1201 New York Ave., NW
Washington, DC 20525
(800) 424-8867
www.nationalservice.org

Society for Nonprofit Organizations
6314 Odana Road, Suite 1
Madison, WI 53719
(800) 424-7367
www.danenet.wicip.org/snpo/

Service Corps of Retired Executives (SCORE)
409 3rd Street, SW 6th Floor
Washington, DC 20024
(800) 634-0245
www. Score.org

United Way of America
701 N. Fairfax Street
Alexandria, VA 22314-7840
(703) 836-7112
www.unitedway.org

Volunteers of America
1660 Duke Street
Alexandria, VA 22314
(703) 341-5000
www.voa.org

YMCA of America
101 N. Wacker Drive
Chicago, IL 60606
(312) 977-0031
www.ymca.org

BOOKS

Beyond Police Checks: the Definitive Volunteer & Employee Screening Guidebook
Linda L. Graff
167 Little John Road
Dundas, Ontario, Canada L9H 4H2
(905) 627-8511
e-mail: ll.graff@sympatico.ca
ISBN: 0-9684760-1-5
1999

The Care & Feeding of Volunteers
Bill Wittich
Knowledge Transfer Publishing
ISBN: 1-928794-10-6
2000

Doing Well, Doing Good Managing Risk in Corporate Volunteer Programs
Nonprofit Risk Management Center
(202) 785-3891
2000

Empower: Child Sexual Abuse Education and Prevention Program
Big Brothers Big Sisters of America
(215) 567-7000
1989

Giving & Volunteering in the United States, 1999 Executive Summary
Independent Sector
ISBN: 0-929556-15-1
(202) 467-6100
1999

The (Help!) I Don't Have Enough Time Guide to Volunteer Management
Katherine Noyes Campbell and Susan J. Ellis
Energize, Inc.
ISBN 0940576-16-3
1995

In Search of America's Best Nonprofits
Richard Steckel
Jossey-Bass Publishers
ISBN 0-7879-0335-3
1997

Kidding Around? Be Serious
Anna Seidman
Nonprofit Risk Management Center
ISBN 0-9637120-3-9
1996

The Ladd Report
Everett Carl Ladd
The Free Press
ISBN 0-684-83735-8
1999

Leading Without Power
Max De Pree
Jossey-Bass Publishers
ISBN 0-7879-1063-5
1997

Managing People Is Like Herding Cats
Warren Bennis
Executive Excellence Publishing
ISBN 0-9634917-5-X
1997

Managing To Have Fun
Matt Weinstein
Simon & Schuster
ISBN 0-684-81848-5
1996

Nonprofit Guide to the Internet
Robin Zeff
John Wiley & Sons, Inc.
ISBN 0-471-15359-1
1996

No Strings Attached: Untangling the Risks of Fundraising & Collaboration
Melanie L. Herman and Dennis M. Kirschbaum
ISBN 1-893210-04-9
Nonprofit Risk Management Center
1999

Planning It Safe: How to Control Liability & Risk in Volunteer Programs
Minnesota Office of Citizenship and Volunteer Services
ISBN: 1-881282-00-7
1998

Semper Fi: Business Leadership the Marine Corps Way
Dan Carrison and Rod Walsh
American Management Association
ISBN 0-8144-0413-8
1999

Staff Screening Tool Kit
John C. Patterson
Nonprofit Risk Management Center,
ISBN 1-893210-00-6
1998

Ten Keys for Unlocking the Secrets to Excellent Volunteer Programs (Audiotape)
Bill Wittich
Knowledge Transfer Publishing
ISBN: 1-928794-09-2
2000

The 21 Irrefutable Laws of Leadership
John C. Maxwell
Thomas Nelson, Inc.
ISBN 0-7852-7431-6
1998

Universal Benefits of Volunteering
Walter Pidgeon
John Wiley & Sons
ISBN 0-471-18505-1
1998

Volunteers for the City
Produced by the Volunteer Exchange of Santa Clara County
A How-to Manual for Developing or Enhancing Municipal Volunteer Programs
Order #05 $25.00
1-800-272-8306

The Volunteer Recruitment Book
Susan Ellis
Energize, Inc.
ISBN 0-940576-18-X
1996

What we learned (the hard way) about Supervising Volunteers
Jarene Frances Lee and
Julia M. Catagnus
Energize Inc.
ISBN 0-940576-20-1
1999

Taking the High Road: A Guide to Effective and Legal Employment Practices for Nonprofits
Jennifer Chandler Hauge and
Melanie L. Herman
ISBN 1-893210-02-2
Nonprofit Risk Management Center
1999

CATALOGS

Volunteer Marketplace 2000
Points of Light Foundation
1400 I Street, Suite 800
Washington, DC 20005
(800) 272-8306
www.PointsofLight.org

Volunteer Energy Resource Catalog
Energize, Inc.
5450 Wissahickon Ave
Philadelphia, PA 19144-5221
(800) 395-9800
www.engergizeinc.com

NATIONAL CONFERENCES

International Conference of Volunteer Administration
(annual conference of the Association for Volunteer Administration)
www.avaintl.org

National Community Service Conference (Points of Light)
(an annual conference in collaboration with the Corporation for National Service, America's Promise and United Way of America)
202-729-8000
www.pointsoflight.org

Nonprofit Risk Management Institutes
(national and regional training seminars held in various geographic locations)
For more information go to their web site at
www.nonprofitrisk.org
or call (202) 785-3891

RISK MANAGEMENT TOOLS

To track the current status of any pending legislation online:
www.thomas.loc.gov
or for more information, call
John Patterson at (202) 785-3891
E-mail : John@nonprofitrisk.org

SUBSCRIPTIONS

Grapevine: *Volunteerism's Newsletter* (bi-monthly)
Steve McCurley and
Sue Vineyard
CAHHS
Volunteer Sales Center
916-928-3950

The Journal of Volunteer Administration (quarterly)
Association For Volunteer
Administration
PO Box 32092
Richmond, VA 23294
(804) 346-2266

Volunteer Leadership
(quarterly)
Points of Light,
1400 I Street NW, Suite 800
Washington, DC 20005
(202) 729-8118

THE WORLD WIDE WEB

www.avaintl.org
(Assoc. Volunteer Administration)

www.charitychannel.com
(Charity Channel)

www.charityvillage.com
(Charity Village)

www.cybervpm.com
(Cyberspace Volunteer Program Management)

www.energizeinc.com
(Energize Inc.)

www.helping.org
(One-stop way to find volunteer opportunities)

www.idealist.org
(Access to 20,000 nonprofit and community organizations)

www.joinhandsday.org
(Americs's Fraternal Benefit Societies)

www.makeadifferenceday.com
(USA Weekend Make A Difference Day Annual Challenge)

www.nutsbolts.com
(Nonprofit Nuts and Bolts)

www.pointsoflight.org
(Points of Light)

www.serviceleader.org/vv/
(Virtual Volunteering)

www.volunteermatch.org
(VolunteerMatch)
Unites volunteers with nonprofits in cities nationwide

www.volunteerpro.com
(Knowledge Transfer)

About the Author

Dr. Bill Wittich is a speaker, consultant, and coach in the field of leadership, motivation, and non-profit management.

Bill earned his doctorate from the University of Southern California, and taught for 31 years at California State University, Long Beach. He served as the department chair for both the Departments of Film & Electronic Arts and Occupational Studies.

For the past ten years Bill and his wife Ann, have traveled an average of 250 days a year. Their speaking schedule has taken them to all corners of the United States and through much of Europe. They speak to non-profit organizations, government agencies, and professional associations.

In 1990, they launched Knowledge Transfer Publishing, a training and publishing organization producing training resources for the non-profit arena. Their first book, The Care & Feeding of Volunteers, is now in its second printing and continues to sell around the world. Their audio cassette album, Ten Keys for Unlocking the Secrets to Excellent Volunteer Programs, has been a best seller in the non-profit field.

Wittich is a professional member of the National Speakers Association. His client list includes a large number of school districts, hospitals, libraries, police and fire departments, labor organizations, associations, and most of the national non-profit organizations.

They enjoy living in Southern California where they enjoy cooking, collecting antiques, and learning about red wine. Those few days a year that are called off-time will find Bill & Ann rambling through Europe or driving that Corvette that simply sits in the garage.

If you'd like more information about Knowledge Transfer seminars in non-profit management, or to inquire about Bill Wittich speaking to your organization, contact:

Knowledge Transfer
3932 Cielo Place
Fullerton, CA 92835
Phone: 714.525.5469
Fax: 714.525.9352
E-mail: Knowtrans@aol.com
Web: http//www.volunteerpro.com